1st edition, *The Potteries of Sunderland and District,* edited J. Crawley, 1951.

2nd edition, revised, *The Potteries of Sunderland and District,* edited J T. Shaw, 1961.

3rd edition, revised, *The Potteries of Sunderland and District,* edited J.T. Shaw, 1968.

4th edition, revised and extended, *Sunderland Ware: The Potteries of Wearside,* edited J.T. Shaw, 1973 (incorporated *Rhymes and Mottoes on Sunderland Pottery,* edited J. Crawley, 1960).

5th edition, revised and extended, *Sunderland Pottery,* revised J C. Baker, 1984.

Published by Thomas Reed Industrial Press   ISBN 0 900335 77 7
and Tyne and Wear County Council Museums   ISBN 0 905974 15 8

Design and photography by Tyne and Wear County Council Graphics/Photographic Unit.

Typeset and printed by Thomas Reed Printers Limited, Sunderland.

Sunderland Pottery

Revised by John C. Baker, B.A., A.M.A.

 Thomas Reed Industrial Press Limited

 Tyne and Wear County Council Museums

I. JUG.

Creamware, with banding at rim and the inscription "Hylton Lowford Pottery, May 21, 1801", painted in enamels. The piece is decorated in an unusual combination of designs: floral border and views of a wind-mill and (reverse) water-mill painted in enamel colours; and transfer-printed borders and oriental landscape designs in blue. The pot was probably used at Dawson's Pottery to show potential customers the range of decorative techniques available.

Dawson's Low Ford Pottery, dated 1801, ht. 8¾in. (22.3cm).

Sunderland Museum Collection.

Contents

4 Preface

5 Foreword

6 Map showing sites of the Wearside Potteries, c.1860

7 The Wearside Pottery Industry

13 The Manufacture of Sunderland Pottery

17 The Varieties of Sunderland Pottery

29 Histories of the Wearside Potteries:

29 Bridge or 'Jericho' Pottery (later Snowdon and Co.)

32 Burnside's Pottery

32 Deptford or *BALL'S* Pottery

37 High Southwick Pottery

37 Low Ford or *DAWSON'S* Pottery

43 Newbottle Potteries

45 North Hylton Pottery (Hylton Pot Works)

46 Seaham Pottery

47 Sheepfold's or Rickaby's Pottery

48 Sheepfold's Warehouse

48 Silksworth Pottery

49 Southwick or *SCOTT'S* Pottery

56 Southwick Union, later the Wear or *MOORE'S* Pottery

60 St. Bede's Pottery, Richmond St., Monkwearmouth

61 Sunderland or *'GARRISON'* Pottery

68 Sunderland Pottery Co., Millfield, later the Wearside Pottery Co.

71 Appendix I
Reproductions of Sunderland Pottery

73 Appendix II
The Wear Bridge

75 Transfer-printed Designs of the Wear Bridge

93 Appendix III
Transfer-printed Designs used by Scott's Pottery

106 Appendix IV
Rhymes, Mottoes and Designs

135 Bibliography

PREFACE

Sunderland Museum's collection of locally made pottery dates back to 1897 when the first donors included the owners of Ball's, Scott's and Snowdon's potteries. The most notable of many subsequent donations was the gift in 1945 of the Rowland Burdon Collection, started by the builder of the 1796 iron bridge over the Wear. Since 1975 Tyne and Wear County Council Museums have purchased some significant new exhibits with financial assistance from the Friends of Sunderland Museums. Several of these recent acquisitions are illustrated in this book.

This publication is the successor to the booklets in four editions between 1951 and 1973 edited first by Mr. J. Crawley, BA, FMA, and then by Mr. J.T. Shaw, ALA, both Directors of Sunderland Libraries, Museum and Art Gallery. This new edition has been revised and extended by John C. Baker, BA, AMA, Senior Museum Officer (Applied Art) at Sunderland Museum. The design of the book has been carried out by Linda Kay, BA (Hons.), of the County Council's Graphic Design Section. The photography is by Dennis Fitton, LBIBP, Joe Hardy and Gillian Richardson, LBIBP, all of the County Council's Photographic Unit, and others as indicated. John Baker would like to thank Mr. James H. Wilson, BA, FMA, former Director of Sunderland Museum, who was responsible for much of the research in previous editions, and Mr. Tom Corfe, former Lecturer in History at Sunderland Polytechnic, for checking the draft of the booklet and for making helpful comments. Thanks are also due to the Rt. Hon. Michael Jopling, PC, MP, for writing the foreword and to those museums and private collectors who have allowed us to illustrate specimens from their collections.

The main source for the histories of the potteries continues to be the extensive manuscript notes written by J.W. Corder (1837-1953) held in Sunderland Central Reference Library. 'Potteries of Sunderland and Neighbourhood' by W.R. Ball in *Antiquities of Sunderland.* Vol.VII, 1906, pp.35-52, despite many inaccuracies, gives interesting information. A great deal of additional material printed in the fourth edition as footnotes was prepared by Mr. Wilson and has now largely been incorporated in the main text. Mr. Wilson was also responsible for listing the various transfer designs on Scott's tableware and the rhymes, mottoes and verses found on Sunderland pottery which appeared as appendices in the fourth edition. These have been retained in this publication, the section on rhymes, mottoes and verses incorporating new material. Information contained in the article 'The Potteries of the Tyne and Wear and their dealings with the Beilby/Bewick Workshop' by M.A.V. Gill in *Archaeologia Aeliana,* 5th series, Vol.IV, 1976, pp.151-170, has proved to be a valuable new source, especially in connection with the early history of the Low Ford Pottery and in identifying the location of the Southwick Union Pottery.

The publication of this book in an extended form and the introduction of colour plates was made possible by co-operation between Tyne and Wear County Council Museums and Thomas Reed Limited, Sunderland's oldest printing firm which was established in 1782. We hope that the publication will meet the needs of the growing number of people interested in the products of one of Wearside's best known industries. We also hope that it will increase collectors' appreciation of Sunderland creamware and yellow-glazed earthenware as well as the better known pink/purple lustreware.

Councillor Bill Craddock,
Chairman,
Tyne and Wear County Council
Museums and Art Galleries Committee.

Kenneth S. Brunton-Reed,
Chairman,
Thomas Reed Limited.

FOREWORD

I am delighted to be asked to write the foreword to the new book on Sunderland pottery. This is the 5th edition and I rejoice that these publications have become increasingly comprehensive and informative. I believe that this edition will, even more than its predecessors, become the standard work of reference on the products of the Wearside potteries.

The book will be warmly welcomed by the growing number of people world-wide, who share my keen interest in these attractive products. Especially, it will draw attention to the Sunderland Museum's incomparable collection. It is good that John Baker, in carrying out this revision, follows the fine tradition of his predecessors in taking such a close interest in Wearside pottery. We must also be grateful to the old Sunderland firm of Thomas Reed, who have taken so much trouble over publication. It is fascinating that Kenneth Brunton-Reed's family were the original owners of the Southwick Union Pottery.

Coming from an old established Sunderland family, I have known Sunderland pottery around the house all my life. I have often noticed that very many Sunderland émigrés also share a knowledge and interest in the products of the town of their roots. I often ask myself why this interest should exist.

Sunderland pottery is a unique reflection of the political, commercial and social life of the greater part of the nineteenth century. The pottery itself is typical of the functional, unsophisticated products of its day. The decorations commemorate great events like battles and war: recording great occasions and people, both local and national. They enthuse over the great commerce of the North East, such as shipping and the coal trade.

But above all, I like them because they are so attractive. I love the romantic fantasies which appear on so many of the decorations. Perhaps I can indulge myself in my favourite rhyme.

"Here's to the Wind that blows
And the Ship that goes
And the Boy that fears no danger,
A Ship in full sail
And a fine pleasant Gale
And a Girl that loves a Sailor."

The Rt. Hon. Michael Jopling, MP.
31st October, 1983.

HOUSE OF COMMONS
LONDON SW1A 0AA

THE POTTERIES OF WEARSIDE

Note: The extent of the various Wearside communities are shown as they existed circa 1860.

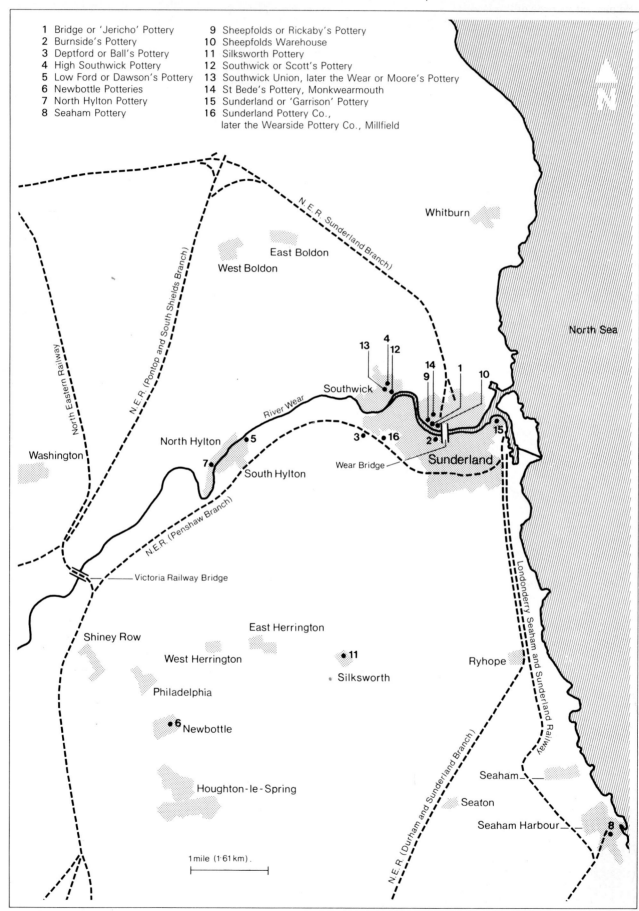

1 Bridge or 'Jericho' Pottery
2 Burnside's Pottery
3 Deptford or Ball's Pottery
4 High Southwick Pottery
5 Low Ford or Dawson's Pottery
6 Newbottle Potteries
7 North Hylton Pottery
8 Seaham Pottery
9 Sheepfolds or Rickaby's Pottery
10 Sheepfolds Warehouse
11 Silksworth Pottery
12 Southwick or Scott's Pottery
13 Southwick Union, later the Wear or Moore's Pottery
14 St Bede's Pottery, Monkwearmouth
15 Sunderland or 'Garrison' Pottery
16 Sunderland Pottery Co.,
   later the Wearside Pottery Co., Millfield

The Wearside Pottery Industry

The earliest records of the Wearside pottery industry relate to Newbottle, a village $4\frac{1}{2}$ miles to the south-west of Sunderland. Here there were deposits of brown clay for the manufacture of coarse-ware and easily worked coal for fuelling the kilns in which the pots were fired. Newbottle is at the edge of the exposed part of the Durham coalfield; eastwards to the coast a capping of magnesian limestone prevented the working of the coal seams until the 19th century when deep mining methods were introduced.

It is possible that pottery for local use was made in Newbottle in the 17th century. Indeed, before the industrial era there were small pottery kilns scattered throughout the region supplying coarse-ware for the local population. There is a reference to 'a kiln' existing in Newbottle in 1615[1], although this may have been a lime kiln and not a pottery kiln. The 'High' Pottery in Newbottle is believed to have been founded just over one hundred years later in 1720. From 1740, after the installation of flint crushing mills at the 'High' Pottery white ware was also made in the village.

During this period pottery-making, which had been a rural craft, was changing into a mass production industry, even though potteries were often operated as family concerns employing small numbers of people. The rising population, more varied diets and the popularity of drinks such as tea and coffee stimulated the production of a greater variety of pots in larger numbers. In order to meet demand pottery-making was increasingly mechanised and potters found it economically advantageous to have their works sited near deposits of clay and coal. Thus Staffordshire which had good quality supplies of both these raw materials became the centre of the English pottery industry. However, ceramics were also made in other coal mining areas such as South Wales, Yorkshire and the North East.

In the second half of the 18th century the North East potteries attempted to emulate wares made further south and imported into the region[2]. In 1765 the 'Low' Pottery at Newbottle advertised ware ''made to as great a perfection as in Staffordshire''[3]. Although the potteries on Wearside may have been influenced by innovations in production techniques and style of decoration, their products never matched the finest ceramics of the South; and North East potteries never succeeded in making porcelain.

Two small potteries were established at Silksworth, near Sunderland, about 1750; but other new potteries which opened in the Wearside area in the 18th century were sited on the banks of the River Wear itself, because it made economic sense. During this period and in the century which followed, the economic development of Wearside centred around the sea trade by which coal was taken from the Wear to London, other east coast ports, and the Continent. Coal mined a few miles inland in the exposed parts of the Durham coalfield was taken by wagonway from places such as Newbottle, Fatfield and Washington, down to the River Wear. There the fuel was loaded on to keel-boats, taken down river and then transferred to coal ships at the mouth of the Wear.

Siting a pottery at the riverside meant that coal could be unloaded from the keel-boats and fed directly into the kilns. Moreover, finished pots were crated and then loaded directly on to ships berthed alongside for convenient transportation to London, principally for export to the Colonies or direct to the countries of North West Europe. Often pottery was sent out

---

1 ''Concerning the barbarous murder near Newbottle'', gives an account of the fatal stabbing of William Watson by Maria Storie at a place called 'Will Surret's kilne'. Hunter's MSS. Dean and Chapter's Library, Bishopric of Durham, quoted in R. Surtees, *The History and Antiquities of the County Palatine of Durham*, vol.1, 1816, p.180.

2 See advertisements of Mary Brougham, *Newcastle Journal*, 3rd June, 1769, and John Jameson, *Newcastle Courant*, 18th May, 1782.

3 *Newcastle Chronicle*, 25th May, 1765.

in colliers, the crates being packed amongst the coal in the hold of the ship. By 1818, 300,000 items of pottery were being exported annually, nearly half to Holland[4].

Along the River Wear brown clay was readily available for the manufacture of coarse-ware, but to emulate the higher quality wares of Staffordshire the Sunderland potteries had to obtain white clay from Devon and Cornwall, and this was brought in at relatively little cost as ballast in the returning coal ships. In the manufacture of creamware and white earthenware the Sunderland potters also required flint. This ingredient added to the whiteness and hardness of the ware and helped to preserve its shape during the firing. The flint from eastern England, south of the River Humber was brought in, again as ballast, in returning colliers. In 1875 Scott's and Moore's were also using flint obtained from France[5].

Probably the first pottery sited by the Wear was at the mouth of the river in Sunderland, close to the pier, and was built before 1753[6]. In January of 1753 a second, newly constructed pottery at Southwick near Sunderland, was advertised[7]. Another pottery was established on the Wear at North Hylton in 1762 by the Maling family. According to family tradition[8] this pottery produced the first transfer-printed ware in the North East but Joseph Warburton, who would have acquired some knowledge of this decorative process during his period of employment at the Bow Factory in London, may well have introduced the technique to the region after moving to Newcastle in 1757[9].

Before 1800 two more potteries were established by the River Wear, one at South Hylton, the other at Southwick: a further seven were opened in the 18th century and one this century. In the late 18th century and the first half of the 19th century pottery-making flourished on Wearside, but then decline set in. Of the original potteries only Ball Brothers' Deptford Pottery and the Bridge Pottery carried on into this century, closing down in 1918 and 1941 respectively. The Wearside Pottery, established in 1913 continued until 1957, although the manager then started a pottery under the same name near Seaham.

During the second half of the 19th century the economic advantages which Sunderland's sea trade had afforded local potters became increasingly irrelevant. Both Ball's Deptford Pottery, re-sited in 1862, and the Sunderland Pottery Co., Millfield, established in 1913, were built, not on the banks of the Wear, but adjacent to the Sunderland-Penshaw-Durham railway which was opened to goods traffic in 1852. Each pottery was served by a siding for the delivery of coal and other raw materials.

The changing character of transport on Wearside was reflected in the attitude of R.T. Wilkinson, a Sunderland solicitor, who operated Moore's Wear Pottery at Southwick from 1861 to 1875. He provided the business with direct access to the Wear by removing substantial ballast hills which stood between the pottery and the river and by building a new quay. Yet he was also aware that the future lay with railways and was one of the main promoters and shareholders of the Monkwearmouth, Hylton and Southwick Railway, opened in 1876, which benefited businesses including Moore's Wear Pottery.

However, Moore's operated for only another six years. By this time the English ceramic industry was centred on the pottery towns of Staffordshire and once a railway network had been established throughout England products from Staffordshire could more easily be sent to the North East. Ball's Pottery for instance took advantage of its direct access to the railway

4   For a table of exports in 1818 see W.R. Ball, 'Potteries of Sunderland and
    Neighbourhood', *Antiquities of Sunderland,* vol.VII, 1906, p.40.

5   See articles on Moore's Wear Pottery and Scott's Southwick Pottery in *Sunderland
    Times,* 4th May and 11th May, 1875.

6   *Newcastle Journal,* 23rd June, 1753.

7   *Newcastle Journal,* 27th January, 1753.

8   L. Jewitt, *The Ceramic Art of Great Britain,* 1878, vol.II, p.8.

9   M.A.V. Gill, 'The Potteries of Tyne and Wear and their dealings with the
    Beilby/Bewick Workshop', *Archaeologia Aeliana,* 5th series, vol.IV, 1976, p.152.

by bringing in items of Staffordshire porcelain for decoration on its premises.

The Sunderland potteries could not match the quality and competitive price of the Staffordshire product, and problems were further compounded by the shortage of skilled labour since in times of 'boom' mines and shipyards paid better wages. Shipyard workers on the Wear were amongst the highest paid skilled artisans in the country. In the 1860s they earned over 30 shillings (£1.50) per week whereas the usual wages of an industrial worker, including those in pottery-making, were well below one pound. William Richard Ball (who became co-owner of Ball's Deptford Pottery in 1884) learned his trade at Rickaby's Pottery, and according to Corder, earned 10s 3d (51p) per week as a thrower on piece work, his name appearing on pay sheets for 1861. Mark Crinson (b. 1841) started a seven year apprenticeship as a thrower at Scott's Pottery in 1859. His indenture in the Sunderland Museum Collection records he started on a wage of 3s 6d (17½p) per week which would rise to 6s (30p) per week in his seventh year of employment.

1. Left: JUG.
Purple lustre, decorated with stylised floral pattern in overglaze enamel and transfer-print, overpainted in enamel colours, of "A View of the Iron Bridge to be erected over the River Thames".
Probably Dawson's Low Ford Pottery, c.1816-19, ht. 6¾in. (17.1cm).
Sunderland Museum Collection.

Right: JUG.
Creamware with painted inscription, "George and Eliza Crothall", and transfer-printed with "A View of the Iron Bridge to be erected over the River Thames", signed "E. Barker, Sunderland", bottom right. The jug is also transfer-printed with view 20 of the Wear Bridge, engraved by Edward Barker.
Probably Dawson's Low Ford Pottery, c.1816-19, ht. 8½in. (21.6cm).
Sunderland Museum Collection.

These two jugs commemorate John Rennie's iron bridge built over the River Thames at Southwark and opened in 1819. A great deal of Sunderland pottery was sent in coal ships to London for re-export to the Colonies and pots such as these were clearly intended for sale in the capital itself.

For a time local and foreign markets ensured that the manufacture of pottery on Wearside continued although on a reduced scale. However, by the late 19th century, to protect their own developing ceramic industry European countries imposed tariffs which restricted the import of English ceramics, except at prohibitively high prices. Scott's Pottery, for instance, formerly carried on a thriving business with Hamburg and other German ports. In 1876 they despatched over thirteen ships laden with white and brown earthenware for delivery for foreign ports. By 1893 Scott's export business was almost confined to Denmark[10]. At this time the Continental ceramic industry had developed to such an extent that the Germans could flood this country with cheap porcelain and examples of such 'export china' exist decorated with views of Sunderland! With the loss of the important European market it was inevitable that the Sunderland pottery industry would collapse.

Both Moore's and Scott's, the two major potteries remaining on Wearside in the second half of the 19th century, were modernised with new buildings and equipment but these improvements failed to prevent their closures in 1882 and 1897 respectively. Ball's and the Bridge Potteries (Snowdon & Co.) which did continue into the 20th century were smaller concerns and survived by concentrating on the production of brown ware, primarily for the local market.

Statistical information taken from the 1841, 1851 and 1861 Censuses reflects the changing fortunes of the Wearside pottery industry. 282 workers were employed in 1841, of whom three were women and eleven were children under the age of 14 (five were under 11). Four workers were aged 70 and over. In 1851, at the peak of the industry the number employed had risen to 395, of whom 63 were women and 45 boys and girls below the age of 14 (eight were less than 11 years old). Six workers were 70 or over. In 1861 the numbers employed had dropped to 334. Of these 59 were women and 25 were children below the age of 14 (one was less than 11 years old). Increasingly the industry recruited immigrant labour including workers born in Ireland, Scotland and a fair number from the pottery towns of Staffordshire. In 1841 52 workers came from outside County Durham (of these eight were Irish and thirteen Scottish). By 1851 the figure had risen to 203 representing over half the workforce and of these 42 were born in Ireland and seventeen in Scotland.

These figures should only be regarded as a guide to the numbers employed in the industry. For instance the 1851 Census lists a total of 46 (22 men, thirteen women and eleven boys) employed at the 'High' Pottery in Newbottle alone, yet the returns for this village list only 35 people as being specifically employed as pottery workers. Some described as 'labourers' in the Census, would have been employed in the pottery industry. Interestingly, the oldest employee at the 'High' Pottery in 1851 was aged 84 and in 1841 the firm had an apprentice of 8 years of age.

Some of the young boys and girls working in potteries may well have been workhouse children, apprenticed by the Poor-law Guardians. We know from the Children's Employment Commission (1841) that they worked a twelve hour day from 6.00 am to 6.00 pm (including one and a half hours for meals) but many often carried out overtime. Journeymen throwers, working by the piece, employed whatever children, of whatever age they wished, the pottery owners having little control over the hiring of these children or what they were paid. The children kept the potters supplied with clay and took away pots for firing. Those children employed in glazing pots experienced nausea, headaches, and tiredness due to lead poisoning. If they remained in this particular aspect of the trade they eventually lost the use of their limbs and suffered brain damage. Girls were mostly employed in the transfer-printing of pots. According to Mr. Carr of the Low Lights Pottery, North Shields, who gave evidence to the Commission, the printer (who was paid from 3d (1p) to 9d (4p) a dozen for transfer-printing pots) had to find his own hands; consequently he paid his children so much per week. Girls were allowed 5d (2p) from every

10 *Sunderland Weekly Echo,* 14th July, 1893.

shilling (5p). If he was a good workman the printer earned for himself, £1 10s 0d (£1.50) to £1 12s 0d (£1.60) per week after paying his hands. Carr stated that in the turning department boys aged 11 to 13 were employed to turn lathes. They earned 8 shillings (40p) to 10 shillings (50p) per week.

In the first half of the 19th century Dawson's Pottery at South Hylton was a major employer. A note found in a foundation stone of the chimney of the flint crushing mill erected at the pottery in 1840 stated that about 200 hands were employed by the firm. According to the 1851 Census there were 107 people living in South Hylton who were employed in the pottery industry. In the second half of the 19th century large numbers of pottery workers were employed at Moore's and Scott's. After improvements to its works in the 1860s Moore's was capable of employing 250 hands, when operating at full capacity. Most were women engaged in more delicate work such as pot decoration. Scott's employed 138 persons in 1851, rising to 152 in 1861. In 1878 Scott's employed 150, many of them having worked for the firm for over 50 years. Manuscript lists from Scott's reveal a family tradition of working at the pottery with three generations commonly employed. In 1969 Sunderland Museum had an enquiry from a Mr. Robert Crinson of Castleford, then aged 94, who had been employed as a thrower at Snowdon's Pottery after serving his apprenticeship at Sheepfolds Pottery. His family had all worked at Scott's Pottery, the first member who could be traced being William Crinson who joined the firm in 1788 and worked there until his death in 1836.

The Scott family, who operated Southwick Pottery from 1788 to 1897, were large landowners in Southwick, and also owned the nearby Southwick Bottle Works. Most of the other Sunderland pottery owners were not prominent business men, merely skilled craftsmen who operated their businesses as small family concerns. By contrast the owners of glass works and shipyards tended to be wealthy men who played a prominent part in the public life of Sunderland. Their social position reflected the importance of these two industries in comparison to pottery-making. Whereas the Census returns for 1841, 1851 and 1861 show the numbers employed in pottery-making rising from 282 to 395 then falling to 334, the numbers employed in the local glass industry show a steady rise from 312 to 716 to 1,105. Even the latter figure is small in comparison to the 7,500 (of Sunderland's total population of over 80,000) employed in the 1860s in the shipbuilding and associated marine industries, by far the largest trade on Wearside.

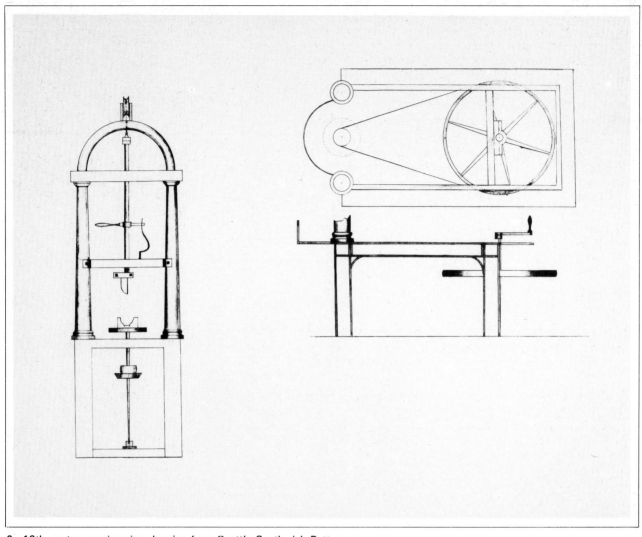

2. 19th century engineering drawing from Scott's Southwick Pottery.
Showing hand-operated jolly for shaping hollow wares such as cups and bowls. Boys were employed to turn the large wheel which powered the revolving table on which the mould was placed.

Sunderland Museum Collection.

The Manufacture of Sunderland Pottery

Most Sunderland jugs, mugs and bowls were thrown, *i.e.,* shaped on the potter's wheel. The throwing rings left by the fingertips of the potter can often be seen on the inside of pieces. Once the pot had been shaped the clay was left to dry to a 'leather-hard' state. It was then turned to a smooth finish using metal or wooden tools.

The handles of jugs and mugs were pulled or extruded. The former type was shaped by the potter using his thumb and index finger, from a sausage of clay. The pulled handle (which can be found on Sunderland creamware of the late 18th and early 19th centuries) tapers towards its base. The extruded handle, however, has a uniform thickness because it was shaped from clay which had been forced through a hole in metal using a plunger system. Such handles are found on the typical Sunderland lustre jug.

Sunderland potters occasionally shaped their ware by pressing thin slabs of clay into or on top of plaster moulds. Large oval dishes and plates could be made in this way either by draping the clay over convex moulds which formed the inside of the article or by pressing the clay into a concave mould which formed the outside of the article. Jugs with multifaceted sides were formed by the clay being pressed into two-piece moulds. When the clay had dried out and separated from the mould the halves of the jug were glued together using slip (clay watered down to the consistency of thick soup).

Pots and handles of a more complicated shape were made by slip-casting. The slip was poured into a plaster mould and this absorbed the water and left a layer of clay to dry on the surface of the mould. The surplus slip was poured away. After drying to a 'cheese-hard' state the clay article was removed from the mould which could be in two or more sections (Fig. 3).

Saucers, tea and dinner plates were made on a jigger. A pancake of clay was draped over a mould placed on a revolving wheel. The clay was then pressed against the mould by a lowered tool or 'profile' (fastened to an arm or counter-balance) which cut away excess clay and shaped the outside of the plate, the mould forming the inside.

Often the Sunderland potters used a jolly to shape cups and bowls. The device worked on the same principle as the jigger but the mould formed the outside of the pot and the tool or 'profile' formed the inside (Fig. 2).

Before they were fired pots were left to dry and harden thoroughly. They were then placed in saggars (vessels made from fire-clay which preserved the shape of the pots and protected them from flames and smoke during firing), and these were then stacked in kilns, which in the 18th and 19th centuries were coal fired and often bottle shaped. The constricting neck of this type of kiln restricted heat loss and encouraged the upward flow of air giving better combustion.

Only earthenware was made on Wearside. Such ware was fired for about 48 hours at a temperature around 980°C. The pots were in a 'biscuit' state after their first firing. They were decorated and glazed and fired for a second time at lower temperatures (about 900°C) in a glost kiln. Subsequent decoration might demand a third or even more firings (at about 700°C) in a muffle kiln.

Transfer-printing was the type of decoration most commonly used by the Sunderland potters. A design was engraved upon a copper plate from which any number of impressions could be taken on moistened plain paper. The paper was then pressed and rubbed on the surface of the pot and this transferred the inked design from the paper (see Fig. 4).In under-glaze printing a design was transferred directly onto the 'biscuit' (*i.e.,* the pot after its first firing). The pot was given a short low-temperature firing which knit the inked design to the surface of the pot, which was then glazed and re-fired, this time in a glost kiln. In overglaze printing the pot had already been glazed and fired before the transfer-print was applied. A third firing in a muffle kiln was required to secure the colour to the glaze. Because they were not protected by the glaze 'over-prints' were easily scratched.

3. JUG.
Unfired grey clay and base and one half of the plaster mould in which the jug was shaped by slip-casting.

Wearside Pottery Co., c. 1939, ht. (of jug) 5in. (12.7cm).

Sunderland Museum Collection.

W.R. Ball of the Deptford Pottery gave the following description of transfer-printing on pottery:

"First the Copper Plates are heated then the colouring is smeared over the engraving with a pallet knife, after which it is scraped off; the plate then being rubbed with a pad made from corduroy so as to remove any surplus.

Next damp tissue paper is placed upon the plate which is then run several times through a heavy metal rolling press (much the same in design as an old-fashioned mangle) the rollers being covered with two or three layers of very thick felt.

Then the plate is again placed upon the hot stove. This dries the paper which is then removed, leaving the imprint from the copper plate upon it, then placed upon the pottery which is sometimes in the Biscuit but more often in the Glazed state; next we require a rubber this being made by rolling felt round and round until it is about 2½ in. dia. and 6 in. long this being used to transfer the design from the paper to the pottery by rubbing after which they (the pieces) are placed in a bath for water to soften the paper which is then easy to remove. Next we have to place the ware in a kiln or oven so as to remove all traces of oil from the print and at the same time make it adhere firmly to the articles after which it is often painted by hand then again placed in the kiln."

4. PLATE.
Transfer-printed with 'Haddon Hall' design in purple. A copper plate engraved with the 'Haddon Hall' design is shown, left, with a paper 'pull' (mounted on card for display purposes) which transferred the ink from the copper plate to the pot. Note that the various parts of the pattern on the 'pull' had to be cut out before application, the factory/pattern mark at the bottom being applied to the base of the plate and that the inked image was reversed out when transferred to the pot.
Impressed mark: SCOTT.
Printed mark: HADDON, S. B. & Co.
Scott's Southwick Pottery, c. 1850-80, dia. 9⅝in. (24.4cm).
Sunderland Museum Collection.

Sunderland potters used gold (copper), purple and silver lustre to decorate their pots. If gold lustre is applied to a brown surface a copper colour results: if applied to a white background the lustre fires to a colour ranging from light pink to deep purple, depending on how thickly the lustre has been applied and the temperature of the firing. Potters obtained a copper lustre finish on white earthenware by painting a layer of brown slip on to the pot and this served as a background for the application of the lustre solution. This technique was used in the manufacture of purple lustre religious plaques which have copper lustre borders. Silver lustre has the brilliance of actual silver but is made from platinum.

John Hancock (1758-1857), an enameller and ceramic chemist, developed a process which made metallic lustre decoration on pottery commercially feasible. Whilst employed at the Staffordshire factory of Spode in 1805 he experimented with platinum, then known as platina. The metal was first discovered in the Spanish Colonies of South America and became known in Europe around 1750. Until the early 19th century, however, the metal remained scarce. In 1805 Hancock introduced steel lustre and shortly afterwards John Gardner of Stoke had the idea of adding a second coating of platinum to produce silver lustre. Gold or copper lustre appeared during 1806.

The secret of lustre spread rapidly and was employed first in the Staffordshire industry and then in other ceramic manufacturing areas. Gold and silver lustre recipes were recorded by Thomas Lakin, a native of Staffordshire, who went to the Leeds Pottery and introduced the lustre process there about 1808-10. In 1824 Lakin's widow published 136 lustre recipes under the title of *Pottery Enamelling and Glass Staining. The Valuable Receipts of the Late Thomas Lakin*[11].

During the 19th century the Sunderland potters used the following formula for gold, commonly called copper lustre:
5 parts powdered gold with the addition of a little tin were dissolved in 30 parts hydrochloric acid and 10 parts of nitric acid. This process took about two hours. Separately 30 parts of balsam of sulphur (4 parts crystallised sulphur, 8 parts turpentine and 16 parts linseed oil) and 20 parts of turpentine were mixed and gently heated. To this diluted boiling solution was added the gold solution. By this time the percentage of gold in the solution was only about 3 per cent. The cost of the metal for covering an average pot was less than one penny (0.4p).

The gold lustre mixture was applied to the already glazed pot with a fine brush moistened with turpentine. The pot was then re-fired in a muffle kiln. The temperature at firing was comparatively low to ensure that the already applied glaze would not melt. During firing the sulphur burnt away thus absorbing oxygen which helped to reduce the gold covering to a metallic state.

In the production of pink or purple lustre Sunderland potters used the same process as gold lustre except that the solution was applied to pottery of a cream or white body. The lustre was often applied with broad brush strokes, the decorator creating panels which were left free for painted enamel inscriptions or patterns or transfer-printed designs and verses. The speckled or mottled effect on Sunderland lustreware was achieved by spraying spirits of turpentine through a tube, covered at the end with fine muslin. The tiny droplets burst upon the still wet lustre coating, forming irregular spots.

For silver lustre potters used platinum, again dissolved in hydrochloric and nitric acids in the proportions of 5:30:10. This solution was then added to 135 parts of spirits of tar and the mixture applied to the glazed pottery. The spirit of tar carbonised during the re-firing and absorbed oxygen, creating a reducing atmosphere which converted the platinum mix to a metallic film on the surface of the pot. A second coating usually composed of dilute platinum oxide and another firing were required to achieve a brilliant silver-like sheen.

The Sunderland potters often painted inscriptions, and free-hand designs (such as floral patterns), or embellished transfer designs with enamel colours. These were fired on to the glazed surface of a pot at low temperatures (up to 700°C) so that the glaze would not melt. The actual enamels comprised a glassy mixture coloured with metallic oxide. Purples derived from manganese, reds and browns from iron oxide, green from copper, blue from cobalt, yellow from antimony. These oxides were also used to colour glazes (see Pl. II, p.18) though in the main Sunderland potters used a transparent glaze (sand mixed with lead oxide) on their wares in order to make them waterproof and to give them a brilliant surface.

11 For a historical and technical account of lustre decoration on ceramics see U. Des Fontaines, *Wedgwood Fairyland Lustre*, 1975, Chap.1.

5. QUART MUG.

Decorated with purple lustre banding and transfer-print of the "Sunderland Lifeboat" signed "Cockburn" bottom right. Beneath the design "R. Scott" is painted left and "N.B." right of the title box. The significance of this is unknown. To the left of the transfer is the North Pier Lighthouse, erected in 1802 and demolished in 1902. Its prominent weather vane is in Sunderland Museum.

Probably Sunderland ('Garrison') Pottery, c. 1820, ht. 4⅝in. (11.7cm).

Sunderland Museum Collection.

6. QUART MUG.

Decorated with purple lustre banding and transfer-print of 'The Sailor's Farewell', signed "Downing Sculpt"., bottom right. This may be the work of William Downing, an engraver known to be working in Staffordshire, c. 1800-11. Another version of the 'Sailor's Farewell' is shown in Fig. 53, p.52.

Printed mark: DIXON, AUSTIN & CO., SUNDERLAND.
Sunderland ('Garrison') Pottery, c. 1820-26, ht. 5in. (12.7cm).

Sunderland Museum Collection.

7. WALL PLAQUES.

Purple lustre, decorated with copper lustre borders and transfer-printed religious verses and mottoes, and known in the trade as 'scripture titles'.

Impressed mark: (plaques, left and centre) DIXON & CO.; (plaque, right) DIXON, PHILLIPS & CO. (surrounding anchor).
Sunderland ('Garrison') Pottery, c. 1820-65, ht. 7¾in. (19.7cm).

Sunderland Museum Collection.

The Varieties of Sunderland Pottery

The products of the Wearside potteries wére considerable, varying in quality and type including coarse brown kitchenware, creamware, printed tableware, copper, silver, and pink/purple lustre. The range of articles covered dinner services, tea-sets, jugs, mugs, bowls, plaques, ornamental tiles, figures, etc. Most of the output of the potteries was transfer-printed tableware for the local population and for markets in Europe and the Colonies. Their most famous product was the transfer-printed pink/purple lustreware now keenly collected throughout the world. Such pottery is known as 'Sunderland Ware', a generic term which is highly misleading because it gives the impression that purple lustre was the only type of pottery made on Wearside and moreover that purple lustreware was made only in Sunderland, whereas, in fact, the type was produced in all major pottery-manufacturing areas throughout the country.

Sunderland creamware and pink/purple lustreware are characterised by the particular subject matter of the transfer designs. These were of great variety including designs, mottoes, and delightfully quaint verses relating to seafaring, religion and politics (Figs. 5 -9). The most popular design was the famous Wearmouth Bridge, described in Appendix II. These transfer-printed pots can be regarded as 'souvenirs' purchased to some extent by local people but in the main by the merchants and seamen who visited Sunderland. A great deal of Sunderland pink/purple lustre can still be found all over eastern England and in the south-west peninsula, as well as throughout the former British Empire; this reflects the sea trade of Sunderland during the 19th century.

The Sunderland potteries catered mainly for people with moderate incomes. Transfer-printed creamware and pink/purple lustreware were made not for artistic effect but with a view to quick sales. The pottery was required to have popular appeal with the result that decorations and verses are frequently typical of the somewhat broad and grim humour of the period (Fig. 8). Frog-mugs made from the late 18th century to the late 19th century proved to be very popular. Other interesting pink/purple lustreware included jugs in sets of 12 in varying sizes, the smallest the size of a cream jug, the largest of 2½ gallons (11.4 litres) capacity; and sets of 12 bowls, each with a transfer depicting a month of the year.

Pottery was frequently made to special order for presentation purposes to celebrate such occasions as birthdays, baptisms and weddings. Other

9. MUG.
Creamware, decorated with transfer-printed portrait of Sir Francis Burdett (1770-1844), M.P. ''The Independent Champion of British Freedom''. Burdett was a populist politician. He advocated parliamentary reform, Catholic emancipation, freedom of speech, prison reform and other liberal measures. In 1810 he was imprisoned for a few days after declaring the conduct of the House of Commons illegal in imprisoning a radical orator. In 1820 he was fined £1,000 and imprisoned for three months after criticising the 'Peterloo Massacre'.

Printed mark: JOHN PHILLIPS & CO., SUNDERLAND POTTERY.
Sunderland ('Garrison') Pottery, c. 1810-20, ht. 5¼in. (13.3cm).

Sunderland Museum Collection.

8. CHAMBER POT.
Purple lustre, transfer-printed with the humorous verse 'Marriage', and on the inside a frog with a transfer-printed seated figure exclaiming, ''Oh! Dear Me! What Do I See?'' with the rhyme;

"Keep me Clean and use me well,
And what I see I will not tell''.

Note that modern reproductions of such pots can often be found.
Probably Sunderland ('Garrison') Pottery, c. 1840, dia. 8½in. (21.6cm).
Sunderland Museum Collection.

10. BOWL.
Purple lustre, decorated with various transfer-printed designs, including a portrait of Garibaldi (1807-82), the Italian soldier and patriot who helped create an independent and united Italy.

Impressed mark: DIXON & CO (used indiscriminately from 1813).
Sunderland ('Garrison') Pottery, c. 1860, dia. 11¼in. (28.6cm).

Sunderland Museum Collection.

II. SPILL VASE, INKSTAND AND VASE.
Decorated with coloured glazes, (spills are thin strips of wood or twisted paper for lighting candles, pipes, etc.).

Snowball's St. Bede's Pottery, c. 1885, ht. (of vase) 7⅞in. (20cm).

Sunderland Museum Collection.

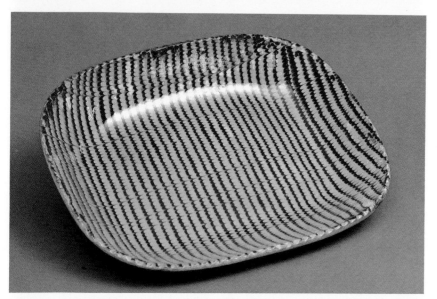

III. LARGE DISH.
Decorated with 'combed' slip.

Impressed mark: SCOTT'S WARRANTED FIREPROOF.
Scott's Southwick Pottery, c. 1850-97, length 20¾in. (52.7cm).

Sunderland Museum Collection.

IV. Left: CRADLE.
'Marbled Ware', with handles and lions' faces in relief in white earthenware.

Glaholm and Robson's Bridge ('Jericho') Pottery, c. 1880, ht. 8in. (20.3cm).

Sunderland Museum Collection.

Right: MONEY POT.
'Marbled Ware', made by David Birney, aged 14, when an apprentice at the Bridge ('Jericho') Pottery.

Patterson's Bridge ('Jericho') Pottery, c. 1890, ht. 5in. (12.7cm).

Sunderland Museum Collection.

V. COFFEE POTS.
Transfer-printed with 'Paisley' pattern in yellow slip.
Scott's Southwick Pottery, c. 1850, ht. (of pot, right) 10in. (25.4cm).
Sunderland Museum Collection.

VI. Left: CHRISTENING MUG.
Creamware, with banding at rim, lettering and floral design painted in enamel colours. The piece is much restored.

Probably Maling's North Hylton Pottery, dated 1793, ht. 6½in. (16.5cm).

Sunderland Museum Collection.

Right: MARRIAGE MUG.
Creamware, with banding at rim, dedication, verse and floral pattern painted in overglaze enamels.

Probably Phillips' North Hylton Pottery, dated 1824, ht. 4¾in. (12.1cm).

Sunderland Museum Collection.

Sunderland products of special interest are pot eggs (Figs. 21, 36), carpet balls (Fig. 89) and bachelor's supper sets; these consist of plate, tobacco or biscuit barrel, goblet, candle and snuffer, which stack one on top of the other and were intended to demonstrate the skill of the thrower (Pls. X, p.23 and XIII, p.27). The best work of the Sunderland potteries is noted for good design and decoration, while nearly all examples possess a certain charm. Most pieces have a freshness and spontaneity of style which is very appealing.

The main categories of Sunderland pottery can be summarised as follows:

BROWN WARE, SLIPWARE AND MARBLED WARE

Simple coarse-ware of local brown clay was made at several Wearside potteries. Some items, such as flower pots were left bare, others were glazed to render them impervious to liquids. Jugs and dairy bowls were often given white slip interiors to relieve the starkness of the brown body (Fig. 16), whilst certain items such as divided baking dishes were embellished with trails of white slip in much the same way as cakes are decorated with icing. Scott's Pottery produced large oval baking dishes in fire-proof clay decorated with bands of slip in alternating colours which were combed by having a feather run through them whilst still wet. (Pl.III, p.18). The tradition of making kitchenware in fire-proof clay was continued this century by the Wearside Pottery Co. which produced a wide range or utility ware often decorated in brightly coloured glazes. Occasionally the Sunderland potters made items like money pots in marbled ware by mixing layers of white clay with brown clay (Pl.IV, p.18).

YELLOW TRANSFER-PRINTED BROWN WARE

In the mid-19th century Scott's Pottery produced items such as tiles, fruit dishes and coffee pots in brown earthenware which were decorated with yellow transfer-printed designs including 'Mosaic', 'Basket Weave' and 'Paisley' patterns (Pl.V, p.19 and Fig. 57). Such ware, and indeed other pieces impressed 'Scott', are sometimes attributed to a pottery at Portobello near Edinburgh, said to have been owned by a Scott family between c. 1786-96. Yet, clearly the 'Scott' items are examples of mid-19th century and not late 18th century pottery. Moreover, it has been shown beyond reasonable doubt that a Scott's Pottery in Portobello never existed[12]. Consequently yellow transfer-printed brown ware impressed 'Scott' should always be attributed to Scott's Southwick Pottery on Wearside.

CREAM-COLOURED EARTHENWARE

The Sunderland potteries made this ceramic type, commonly called creamware in the late 18th and early 19th centuries. They produced plain tableware, items such as marriage mugs with painted floral designs in overglaze enamels (Pl.VI, p.19), and jugs and mugs decorated with views of the Wear Bridge of 1796 and other transfer-printed designs (Pl.VII, p.22). This thinly potted and lightweight earthenware with a distinct cream colour was made from Devon pipe-clay mixed with calcined flint and was developed in Staffordshire about 1720. By the late 18th century it had become the staple earthenware product made in all the pottery-making areas throughout the country. The body proved an ideal background for transfer-printed decoration, after the technique had been developed in the 1750s, and for painted enamel designs.

12 P. McVeigh, *Scottish East Coast Potteries, 1750-1840,* Chap. II, 'Scott Brothers — The Phantom Pottery', 1979, pp.122-128. See also articles by G. Cruickshank, in *Scottish Pottery Archive News,* vol.4, 1979, pp.4-10, and *Scottish Pottery Historical Review:* vol.5, 1980, pp.10-18 and vol.6, 1981, pp.76-79.

YELLOW-GLAZED EARTHENWARE

This pottery commonly called 'Yellow Ware' or 'Canary Yellow' is creamware dipped in yellow glaze, the actual colour deriving from antimony oxide (Pl.VIII, p.22). It was made in the period 1780-1835 at many potteries throughout the country, including Wearside. Examples which can definitely be attributed to Sunderland are rare, but marked pieces, decorated with transfer-printed designs made at Dawson's Low Ford Pottery and the Sunderland ('Garrison') Pottery are known[13].

'GAUDY WELSH'

This term is applied to white glazed earthenware of the period c. 1830-1860 gaudily painted with a particular stylised flower design in orange, blue, and green enamels, and copper lustre. A great deal was exported to America. It was assumed that this type of pottery was made in South Wales only. However, it was certainly made in Staffordshire and the North East, including Wearside. 'Gaudy Welsh' plates impressed 'Dawson' are known (Pl.IX, p.23).

TRANSFER-PRINTED TABLEWARE

The bulk of production from the Wearside potteries in the 19th century consisted of dinner services and tea-sets in white earthenware. This is not generally realised because such ware was made to be used, was often broken and then thrown away. Consequently very little has survived to the present. By contrast the famous Sunderland pink/purple lustreware was normally used for decorative purposes only and a high proportion has remained intact. The abundance of Sunderland lustre gives the mistaken impression that this product and not transfer-printed tableware formed the greater part of the output of the Wearside potteries.

Only rarely was tableware left undecorated. Sometimes items were painted with overglaze enamel floral designs (Pl.X, p.23) but most were transfer-printed. The Wearside potteries used a wide range of designs including 'Willow' pattern, romantic, classical or English landscape scenes and floral patterns. An indication of the variety of designs produced by only one of the major Wearside potteries — Scott's — is given in Appendix III.

Underglaze blue was the most popular colour used but the Wearside potteries also printed in black, sepia, green and lilac (Pls.XI and XII, p.26 and XIII, p.27).

FIGURES

Slip-cast ornamental figures for decorating shelves and mantelpieces were made throughout the 19th century, primarily in Staffordshire, but also in other pottery-making areas including Wearside. Animals, including lions (Fig.II) and sitting spaniels (the latter embellished with large copper lustre spots) are said to have been made in the area, although the dogs in particular are indistinguishable from Staffordshire products. The Wearside potteries may also have produced busts and figures of 19th century personalities, but the most celebrated local examples are the impressed watchstands and the figures of the 'Four Seasons' decorated in polychrome enamels or pink lustre, made at the Sunderland ('Garrison') Pottery (Fig. 88).

11. FIGURE OF A LION.
Glazed white earthenware.
Probably Sunderland ('Garrison') Pottery, c.1820-50, ht. 8¼in. (21cm).
Sunderland Museum Collection.

13   For examples of Sunderland 'Canary Yellow' see J. Jefferson Miller II, *English Yellow-Glazed Earthenware*, 1979.

VII. Left: JUG.
Purple lustre, transfer-printed with a version of the 'Sailor's Farewell' design, overpainted in enamel colours.

Printed mark: SCOTT, SOUTHWICK.
Scott's Southwick Pottery, c. 1820, ht. 9in. (22.9cm).

Sunderland Museum Collection.

Right: MUG.
Creamware, with banding at rim in black enamel transfer-printed with design of a collier-brig overpainted in enamels and ''Success to the Coal Trade''.

Printed mark: DIXON & CO., SUNDERLAND POTTERY.
Sunderland ('Garrison') Pottery, c. 1813-19, ht. 5⅝in. (14.3cm).

Sunderland Museum Collection.

VIII. Left: JUG.
Yellow-glazed earthenware, with banding in black enamel and decorated with a transfer-print of the launch of a naval ship and the verse ''May Carpenters Flourish''.

Probably Dawson's Low Ford Pottery, c. 1800-10, ht. 5in. (12.7cm).

Sunderland Museum Collection.

Right: JUG.
Yellow-glazed earthenware with banding in black enamel and transfer-printed with a design of the 'Tythe Pig', probably engraved at the Beilby/Bewick workshop, Newcastle.

Probably Sunderland ('Garrison') Pottery, c. 1810, ht. 4in. (10.2cm).

Sunderland Museum Collection.

IX. PLATE.
'Gaudy Welsh', the stylised floral pattern painted in purple lustre and enamel colours.

Impressed mark: DAWSON.
Dawson's Low Ford Pottery, c. 1820, dia. 8⅜in. (21.3cm).

Sunderland Museum Collection.

X. Left: BACHELOR'S SUPPER SET.
With banding at rims in enamel colours and transfer-printed with floral patterns overpainted in enamel colours.

Probably Rickaby's Sheepfolds Pottery, dated 1865, ht. 20in. (50.8cm).

Sunderland Museum Collection.

Right: TUREEN.
Painted with floral patterns in overglaze enamels.

Impressed mark: SCOTT.
Scott's Southwick Pottery, c. 1860-80, ht. 7½in. (19.1cm).

Sunderland Museum Collection.

SILVER LUSTRE

In the 19th century brown earthenware was sometimes shaped like actual silver objects such as teapots (Fig. 12), cream jugs, sugar basins and vases, given a silver lustre coating (the chief constituent of which was platinum) and sold as poor man's silver. This type of pottery is unmarked and is difficult to attribute to its place of manufacture. Some silver lustre was made on Wearside, and indeed other pottery-making areas, but most was produced in Staffordshire.

COPPER LUSTRE

Pottery decorated with a coating of minute quantities of gold and other ingredients, applied to a brown surface, is more common than silver lustreware. Again, examples are usually unmarked and attribution is difficult. Although copper lustreware was produced locally it is difficult to distinguish a Wearside example from one made elsewhere in the country.

Copper lustre items could be left plain but it was more usual to decorate them in a variety of ways. Sometimes designs in vivid enamel colours were painted directly on to the copper surface (Fig. 81) or on to a white or single colour background. Copper lustre patterns were also painted on yellow, blue or green panels. White panels, which had been masked from the lustre, could be decorated with painted purple lustre or transfer-printed designs (Fig. 13). Occasionally items were decorated with applied relief painted in enamels or with a 'pebbledash' effect in white clay.

PINK/PURPLE LUSTRE

Sunderland is famous for white earthenware made in the 19th century decorated with pink or purple lustre — so famous, in fact, that the highly misleading term 'Sunderland Ware' is often applied to all varieties of pink/purple lustre. Pink lustre decoration was used in all pottery-making areas of the country, but Sunderland pink/purple lustreware has particular characteristics which easily distinguish the type from lustreware made outside the North East.

Sunderland pink/purple lustreware is usually transfer-printed with designs, verses and mottoes relating to religion, friendly societies, trade, politics and especially seafaring. However, the most popular designs used by local potters were views of the Wear Bridge, either in its original form of 1796 (when opened it was the world's largest single-span cast-iron bridge) or as re-built with its arch widened and 'levelled off'. This work was carried out in 1858/59 under the supervision of Robert Stephenson. Transfers were often coloured with overglaze enamels and pots may have painted verses in black enamel. 'One off' presentation pieces for christenings, weddings and birthdays also carry dedications and the name of the recipient in hand-painted lettering.

Sunderland products can be recognised by their distinctive shape. Jugs have 'ovoid' bodies and 'loop' handles which are also found on mugs. The fact that they were cheaply made souvenir items aimed primarily at local people or visiting sailors is quite apparent. Sunderland pink/purple lustreware was popular in the 1820s, 30s and 40s, and although the product was made into the late 19th century decline in sales was reflected in falling standards of workmanship in both potting and decoration. As a general rule the lighter in weight the article the older it is likely to be.

Sunderland pink/purple lustreware occasionally bears impressed and/or printed maker's marks. Identification through transfers is not always reliable, as some of the early copper plates were purchased by other potteries when the older firms went out of business and firms sometimes interchanged transfers.

Similar pink/purple lustreware was made at the Tyneside and Teesside potteries and if an item is not marked it is very difficult to distinguish

12. TEAPOT.
Silver lustre.

Probably Sunderland ('Garrison') Pottery, c. 1820, ht. 5¾in. (14.6cm).

Sunderland Museum Collection.

13. GOBLET AND JUG.
Copper lustre, painted with 'Cottage Lustre' design in purple on white panels.

Possibly North Hylton Pottery (these two items were attributed to this pottery by W. R. Ball of the Deptford Pottery when he presented them to Sunderland Museum in 1906), c. 1820-40, ht. (of jug) 5¼in. (13.3cm).

Sunderland Museum Collection.

between a Wearside, Tyneside or Teesside product. If an item is decorated with a transfer-print of the Wear Bridge this is no guarantee that the piece is a Sunderland pot. We know from the Beilby/Bewick workshop accounts[14] that soon after the Wear Bridge was opened in 1796 at least two Tyneside potteries were transfer-printing creamware with views of the bridge and undoubtedly this tradition would have continued in the 19th century with the decoration of pink/purple lustreware. A particular style of decoration found on pink/purple lustreware comprises badly executed transfer-printed designs in dark brown ink set within an oval or four-lobed panel delineated by brush strokes in overglaze enamel, approximating to burnt amber in colour, with a border of painted diagonal dashes in green. Often broad brush strokes in yellow enamel are painted above and below the actual transfer. It is probable that items of pink/purple lustreware with this particular style of decoration are Tyneside products and should not be considered as examples of Sunderland pottery (Pl.XIV, p.27).

Pink/purple lustreware made in Staffordshire, South Wales and Yorkshire is usually more finely potted and has better executed painted and transfer-printed designs. These are more wide ranging in subject matter and rarely have a seafaring theme (Fig. 14).

Another type of pink/purple lustre associated with Sunderland is the painted design known as the 'Cottage Lustre' (Pl.XV, p.30). Marked pieces exist indicating that such ware was made on Wearside but this type was also made elsewhere. Moreover, the 'Cottage Lustre' design is often found on porcelain and of course such examples (as indeed any porcelain item) should never be attributed to any of the North East potteries because only earthenware was made in the region. These two types of ceramic body can be identified by holding the pot against a very strong light. If the body is translucent it is porcelain.

ORANGE LUSTRE

Transfer-printed white earthenware embellished with orange lustre was made in the period c. 1860-1890 and is associated particularly with Ball's Deptford Pottery. This firm produced mugs, jugs, bowls and religious plaques (Pl.XVI, p.30) in this type of ware, decorated with transfers relating to seafaring, religion and the Wear Bridge. The quality of potting and decoration of these items is usually extremely poor. Scott's Pottery also used this type of decoration on some transfer-printed items. An impressed bowl[15] from the Low Lights Pottery, North Shields, which otherwise is identical to examples attributed to Ball's Pottery is evidence that orange lustre was also made on Tyneside.

14. JUG.
Purple lustre, painted with overglaze enamel floral pattern and the inscription "Geo. Wright N7 1825". The transfer-printed design of "The Independent Order of Oddfellows" and the verse are overpainted in enamels. "T. Boddeley, enameller, Hanley", is painted in minute lettering within a ribbon below the last line of the verse below the spout.
This Staffordshire jug could easily be mistaken for a Sunderland product. However, the 'semi-scroll' handle, the careful overpainting of the transfer-prints and the high quality of the hand lettering are characteristics not normally found on Sunderland pots.

Staffordshire, dated 1825, ht. 6in. (15.2cm).

Sunderland Museum Collection.

14   M.A.V. Gill, 'The Potteries of Tyne and Wear and their dealings with the Beilby/Bewick Workshop'. *Archaeologia Aeliana,* 5th series, vol.IV, 1976, pp.154, 168.

15   Laing Art Gallery, Newcastle, Collection (Accn. no. E7762). White earthenware bowl, c. 1870, impressed 'John Carr and Sons', decorated with orange lustre, Wear Bridge View, 'The Sailor's Tear', 'Glide on my bark' and other transfer verses.

XI. **EEL PLATES.**
Transfer-printed in blue.
Left: impressed mark: DIXON, AUSTIN & CO.
Sunderland ('Garrison') Pottery, c. 1820-26, dia. 4¼in. (10.8cm).

Sunderland Museum Collection.

Right: impressed mark: DAWSON.
Dawson's Low Ford Pottery, c. 1820, dia. 4in. (10.1cm).

Sunderland Museum Collection.

XII. **MEAT PLATE.**
Transfer-printed with 'Australian' pattern in brown.
Impressed mark: DIXON & CO.
Printed mark: AUSTRALIAN, DIXON PHILLIPS & CO.
Sunderland ('Garrison') Pottery, c. 1834-65, length 19¼in. (48.9cm).

Sunderland Museum Collection.

XIII. Foreground: BACHELOR'S SUPPER SET.
Made, ironically, as a wedding gift for Douglas and Ann Spalding whose names appear on the piece. Transfer-printed in purple.
Probably Dawson's Low Ford pottery, dated 1857, ht. 20½in. (52.1cm).
Sunderland Museum Collection.

Background: MEAT PLATE.
Transfer-printed with romantic landscape design in green.
Impressed mark: DAWSON.
Dawson's Low Ford Pottery, c. 1840-60, length 19in. (48.3cm).
Sunderland Museum Collection.

XIV. Left: JUG.
Purple lustre, decorated with transfer-printed designs overpainted in enamel colours.
Printed mark: DIXON & CO., SUNDERLAND POTTERY.
Sunderland ('Garrison') Pottery, c. 1820, ht. 10½in. (26.7cm).
Sunderland Museum Collection.

Centre: WALL PLAQUE.
With purple lustre rim, transfer-printed with religious motto with a painted border of dashes in green enamel.
Impressed mark: MALING.
Maling's Ouseburn Bridge Pottery, Newcastle, c. 1840, dia. 6⅜in. (16.2cm).
Sunderland Museum Collection.

Right: JUG.
Purple lustre, decorated with designs including view 12 of the Wear Bridge, transfer-printed in dark brown. These are embellished above and below with broad strokes in yellow enamel within painted surrounds in burnt umber and dashes in green enamel. This distinctive style of decoration, often found on purple lustreware, is probably a feature of Tyneside pottery and such examples should not be attributed to Sunderland.
Probably Tyneside, c. 1850, ht. 10½in. (26.7cm).
Sunderland Museum Collection.

27

15. BIRD WATERER.
Glazed brown earthenware.

Snowdon & Co.'s Bridge Potteries, c. 1910,
ht. 9¾in. (24.7cm).

Sunderland Museum Collection.

Histories of the Wearside Potteries

For collectors of Sunderland pottery the histories of Ball's, Dawson's, Moore's, North Hylton, Scott's and the Sunderland ('Garrison') potteries are of particular interest. These firms made a wide range of products, including brown ware, but also creamware and white ware which was often of high quality and frequently marked.

The other Wearside potteries were on a much smaller scale and produced articles, mainly brown ware, of little interest to the collector. Most of these firms did not mark their pottery and those that did, only rarely. Consequently, attribution of products is difficult except in a few cases where the history of an item in the Sunderland Museum Collection is known.

The following histories are arranged alphabetically:

BRIDGE OR 'JERICHO' POTTERY (LATER SNOWDON AND CO.)

Sited near Sheepfolds Pottery on Sheepfolds, Monkwearmouth (see Fig. 45), this pottery, colloquially known as the 'Jericho', was a small concern with two kilns for the manufacture of brown ware. It was thought that the pottery was built by Samuel Moore and Co., of the Wear Pottery, Southwick (see p. 57) and first appears under this name in the 1844 Directory, although the Electoral Register of 1841 lists Samuel Moore in possession of the works. However, a map of 1829 shows a pottery on the same site and an entry in the 1828 Directory gives 'William Barker, Brown ware manufacturer, Monkwearmouth Shore', which may have been the same manufactory.

The Bridge Pottery operated as a branch of the Wear Pottery for the manufacture of brown ware. In 1861 both concerns passed into the hands of a Sunderland solicitor, R.T. Wilkinson. In 1875 he leased the two potteries to Messrs. Glaholm, Robson and Lyall. In 1881, John Patterson, who had been manager on behalf of Glaholm, Robson and Lyall of the Wear Pottery (closed 1882) and the Bridge Pottery, acquired ownership of the latter and operated the concern until about 1896. The Bridge Pottery was then acquired by C.E. Snowdon and Co[16] who also took over Sheepfolds or Rickaby's Pottery in 1900. By 1904 the business was known as Snowdon, Pollock and Snowdon[17] operating as the 'Bridge Potteries' under which titles the firm continued until 1941, the last surviving potteries on the north side of the River Wear.

16. BOWL AND JUG.
Brown earthenware, with white slip and glazed interiors.
Snowdon & Co.'s Bridge Potteries, c. 1910, ht. (of jug) 8⅞in. (22.5cm).
Sunderland Museum Collection.

PRODUCTS
The pottery made some basic domestic items in glazed white earthenware, but produced mainly brown ware such as flower pots and stew dishes. The firm made considerable quantities of ware for the dairy industry (cream pots, dishes, trays, bowls, jugs, starch pans, etc.), for the home market, mainly in the south of England, and for export to Denmark (Fig. 16).

MARKS
Snowdon Bridge Pottery Sunderland (printed; on earthenware hot water bottle in Sunderland Museum Collection).

---

16 C. E. Snowdon was at one time a warehouseman for Moore's Pottery.

17 C. E. Snowdon died in 1906 and his son W. B. Snowdon (the other Snowdon in the partnership) shortly afterwards. Mr. Pollock who had been a partner in the business since 1901, operated the pottery until it closed.

XV. Left: **TEA-BOWL AND SAUCER.**
Painted with 'Cottage Lustre' design in purple lustre.

Impressed mark (saucer): DAWSON. Dawson's Low Ford Pottery, c. 1820, dia. (of saucer) 4¾in. (12.1cm).

Sunderland Museum Collection.

Right: **TEA-BOWL AND SAUCER.**
Transfer-printed with Adam Buck design in red and overpainted in enamel colours and painted with floral surrounds in purple lustre.

Impressed mark (saucer): DAWSON. Dawson's Low Ford Pottery, c. 1820, dia. (of saucer) 4⅝in. (11.7cm).

Sunderland Museum Collection.

XVI. MUG AND WALL PLAQUE.
Both orange lustre. The mug is transfer-printed with religious verse, the surround overpainted in enamel colours. The wall plaque is transfer-printed with religious motto, the surround overpainted in enamel colours.

Probably Ball's Deptford Pottery, c. 1870, ht. (of plaque) 7½in. (19cm).

Sunderland Museum Collection.

XVII. WALL PLAQUE.

Transfer-printed with romantic landscape design overpainted with enamel colours. Incised on reverse "Levi Copeland, Hylton Pottery". According to Census returns Copeland was a 15 year old apprentice in 1841 living at South Hylton. He was born in Burslem, Staffordshire. The signature on this plaque may indicate it was Copeland's first piece on coming out of his apprenticeship.

Dawson's Low Ford Pottery, c. 1845, ht. 9in. (22.9cm).

Sunderland Museum Collection.

XVIII. FROG-MUG AND JUG.

Transfer-printed with designs, some overpainted in enamel colours. Both pieces are embellished with banding in blue enamel and 'zig-zag' patterns painted in crimson, turquoise and pink enamel, a decorative characteristic of Moore's products.

Printed mark (both pieces): MOORE & CO., SOUTHWICK.
Moore's Wear Pottery, jug dated 1836, ht. (of jug) 6½in. (16.5cm).

Sunderland Museum Collection.

BURNSIDE'S POTTERY

In 1850, William Batey Burnside built a pottery on Pemberton's Field, situated on the south side of the River Wear near the north end of Green Street, Sunderland. It produced chimney pots, roof tiles and similar ware. On Burnside's death in 1858, the pottery closed down. The manufactory is mentioned in local Directories (Wheelan's 1856 and Ward's 1858).

W.B. Burnside had earlier come into possession of a property (through his uncle, Robert Batey, who inherited it in 1819), known as the 'school house', 3 Church Lane, Bishopwearmouth, which included 'a yard on the East with a kiln'. This was probably a pottery kiln, which Burnside worked before setting up at Pemberton's Field. The Census of 1841 gives three potters at this address: John Burnside, aged 44; William Burnside, aged 21; and John Naylor, aged 45. The Census of 1851 shows William Burnside still at the same address and to have been born in Newbottle. The Jury List for 1858 gives 'William Batey Burnside, earthenware manufacturer, Church Lane', and 'John Henry Burnside, earthenware manufacturer, of High Street'.

PRODUCTS
Brown ware, roof tiles and chimney pots.

MARKS
It is unlikely that Burnside marked his products.

DEPTFORD OR BALL'S POTTERY

The Deptford Pottery was established in 1857 by William Ball (born in Sunderland in 1817) whose family had a tradition of working in the pottery industry. His father, Thomas, was a potter who originated from Burslem, Staffordshire. William's brother Richard (b. 1819) was also a potter and his son Thomas (b. 1841) was apprenticed to the trade by 1851, when according to the Census they were living at Ford, South Hylton, both presumably employed at Dawson's Pottery. An indenture in the Sunderland Museum Collection indicates that William Ball's cousin, Lees Ball (born 1810 in Swinton, Yorkshire) was apprenticed for six years in 1825 to Dixon, Austin and Co., working at the North Hylton Pottery; his father, Richard, living at Hylton Ferry probably also worked at this pottery. The 1851 Census lists Lees Ball as living at Ford, South Hylton, again presumably working at Dawson's. He died in 1870 and, as with other members of the Ball family, there is no evidence that he worked for his cousin, William, at the Deptford Pottery. From the evidence of Censuses it also appears that Lees Ball had an elder brother, James (born 1806 at Swinton, Yorkshire), also a potter living in Dawson Terrace, South Hylton in 1841. His son James Jnr. (b. 1831) was apprenticed to the trade in 1851.

William Ball himself had trained at Dawson's Low Ford Pottery and in 1852 worked as a potter in Norway at the 'Ekersunds Store Pottery', founded by Johann Feyer at Jaeren. Ball's agreement, signed 26th July, 1852 (Sunderland Museum Collection) shows him employed as a 'thrower of brown ware and to make himself useful in the pottery' at a wage of 36 shillings (£1.80) per week, with additional payments for other duties, free coal, his personal taxes paid, allowance for house and free passage home for himself and family on termination. The agreement was for two years, with three months' notice on either side.

On returning to England, William Ball then seems to have worked a pottery at West Cornforth, Co. Durham, leased from Mary Lammas in 1855[18]. In the agreement (which is unsigned, with the actual day and

---

18 Little is known of this pottery. An entry in Durham Poll-Book 1832-3 gives 'Thomas Lammas, Coxhoe Pottery'. The 1856 Directory shows 'Mary Lammas, Farmer, Cornforth': 'Harrison Row, tobacco pipe manufacturer at the Cornforth Pottery' and states "The village comprises two corn mills, a brick and tile manufactory and a pottery".

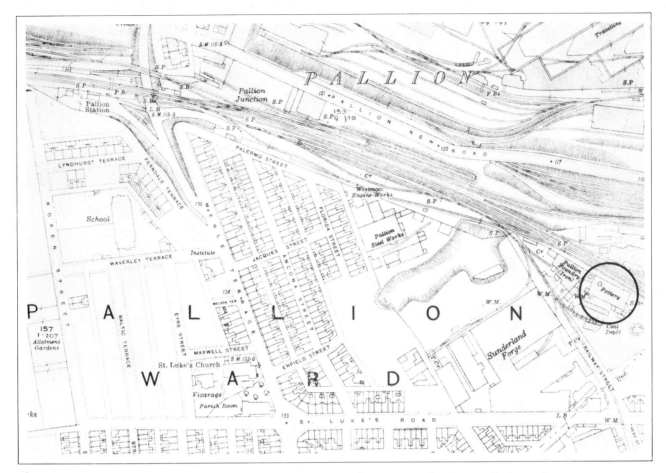

17. Detail of map showing the Deptford Pottery sited alongside the Sunderland — Penshaw — Durham railway.
Ordnance Survey Map, scale: 25 inches to 1 mile, 1919 edition. Durham Sheet VIII, 13.

month left blank), now in the Sunderland Museum Collection, Ball is described as 'of Newcastle upon Tyne' and intended the manufacture of 'brown ware pots, pot pipes and chimney pots'. If Ball did operate this pottery it could only have been for two years, before he set up his own business named the Deptford Pottery (a small concern for the manufacture of brown ware and flower pots) at Diamond Hall, Deptford, Sunderland.

In 1862, due to increased demand for his wares, Ball moved to new and larger premises built adjacent to the Sunderland-Penshaw-Durham railway, opened to goods traffic in 1852. The pottery had a siding by which raw materials could be taken directly in (Fig. 17). This was especially convenient because the pottery, in addition to brown ware, now also produced white earthenware using Devon clay and purchased already manufactured pottery and porcelain from Staffordshire, for decoration. Brown ware was made from local clay obtained from a site nearby belonging to John Candlish, a local glass bottle manufacturer. In 1875 a further extension to the Deptford Pottery was made, including a second furnace, new workshops and warehouses. According to Directories of 1873 and 1879 William Ball was also in business at South Hylton, described as 'earthenware manufacturer and brickmaker'. The firm also sold ground flint and china stone[19]. Presumably Ball was operating the Bank Top Pottery (Fig. 27) and the flint crushing mill originally operated by the Dawson family (p.37).

After William Ball died in 1884 the Deptford Pottery was managed by his two sons William Richard (1842-1918) and Thomas Lees[20] trading as Ball Brothers. The former had trained at Rickaby's Pottery. He was an

19 Advertisement in *Pottery Gazette,* 2nd January, 1882.
20 His daughter, Miss Florence Ball (1873-1971), lived in Sunderland and as well as providing much valuable assistance with regard to the family pedigree, presented to Sunderland Museum documentary evidence, specimens of the firm's pottery and one of the copper transfer plates used there.

enthusiast on matters concerning the Wearside pottery industry and presented a paper on the subject to the Sunderland Antiquarians in 1906. After the death of W.R. Ball his brother Thomas retired from the business and the Deptford Pottery was closed down and dismantled in 1918.

18. FROG-MUG.
Decorated with banding in purple enamel and transfer-prints.
Ball's Deptford Pottery, c. 1890, ht. 5⅜in. (13.6cm).
Sunderland Museum Collection.

PRODUCTS

In addition to brown ware the pottery produced a considerable amount of white earthenware including jugs, mugs and bowls decorated with transfers from copper plates purchased from the 'Garrison', Moore's and Scott's potteries on their closure. Such transfers were printed in not only the normal black, but also in blue, green and brown. Sometimes the transfers were used in conjunction with pink/purple lustre but more often with orange lustre (Pl. XVI, p.30). Ball's continued to make transfer-printed lustreware into this century. Where the copper plate bore, as part of the transfer, the name of the pottery which originally owned it, Ball's rarely bothered to erase it and this causes confusion in attribution. Corder noted that a remonstration to W.R. Ball on this point brought the rejoinder that, as he had bought both the plates and the rights, he was perfectly justified, as the proprietor of an old Sunderland firm, in leaving the names on, if people would buy the goods. When Ball's Pottery closed, most of these copper plates were sold (Corder thought to a Yorkshire concern), but a few remained in the family. Three were presented to Sunderland Museum in 1963 by Mr. John Ball, a grandson of Thomas Lees Ball. As reproduction Sunderland lustreware has appeared on the market, it may well be that some of the plates are still in use (see Appendix I). Should named transfers occur in conjunction with either coloured transfer-printing and/or orange lustre the examples can be attributed to the Deptford

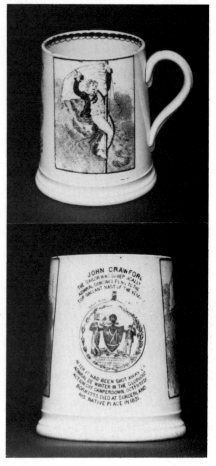

19. MUG.
Decorated with John ('Jack') Crawford transfer-prints. Crawford (1775-1831) born in Sunderland, the son of a keelman, went to sea when he was about eleven. He later joined the Royal Navy and served on Admiral Duncan's flagship 'Venerable'. In 1797 Duncan engaged the Dutch fleet off Camperdown, Holland. During the battle the top of 'Venerable's' mainmast was shot down, bringing with it the Admiral's colours. To avoid confusion, since the English fleet may have believed Duncan had surrendered, Crawford climbed the stump of the main mast and nailed the Admiral's flag to it. Eventually the English fleet won a great victory.
Crawford became a folk-hero on his return to Sunderland. Through public subscription the town raised money for a silver medal to be made and this was presented to Jack in March 1798. One of the transfer-prints on this mug depicts this medal which is now in Sunderland Museum. Crawford took up work as a keelman, but despite this and a pension of £30 per year which he eventually received from the Navy, he spent the rest of his life in some poverty. Crawford died 10th November 1831, an early victim of the terrible cholera epidemic which struck Sunderland.

Ball's Deptford Pottery, c. 1870-90, ht. 5in. (12.7cm).

Sunderland Museum Collection.

Pottery. Moreover, Ball's products are often extremely badly executed, having thickly potted walls and bases, smudged transfer-printing and clumsily painted lustre and/or enamel decoration.

Ball also secured from the 'Garrison' pottery the moulds for the manufacture of 'Sunderland' lions. These were reproduced at the factory but the large fangs of the originals were replaced by small, rather evenly sized 'kitten' teeth.

Two registered transfer designs showing Jack Crawford, the local hero of the Battle of Camperdown of 1797 (Figs. 19 and 20) were used by the firm in the late 19th century. Often the designs were printed on porcelain brought in from Staffordshire.

The Deptford Pottery also produced drawer-knobs in black glazed earthenware, with china centres painted with floral designs. Several pot-painters[21] were employed by the firm to decorate breakfast and dessert sets, jugs, etc., or articles to customer's special requirements (Fig. 21). Again, such items could include porcelain made in Staffordshire.

MARKS
Copyright Ball Bros. Sunderland (printed on 'Jack Crawford' design).

20. Left: JUG.
Decorated with gilding and 'Jack Crawford' transfer-print in brown overpainted in enamel colours.

Ball's Deptford Pottery, c. 1870-90, ht. 9in. (22.9cm).

Private Collection.

Right: PLATE.
Staffordshire porcelain, decorated at Ball's Deptford Pottery. The openwork rim is painted with blue enamels, with the 'Jack Crawford' design transfer-printed in brown.

Printed mark: COPYRIGHT BALL BROTHERS SUNDERLAND.
Staffordshire, c. 1870-1900, dia. 9¼in. (23.5cm).

Sunderland Museum Collection.

21 A catalogue of a Trades Exhibition held in Sunderland in 1887 lists the following:
 Miss E. Donkin, Miss E. Woodhill, Miss M. Downies and Mr. L. Olson.

21. CHRISTENING EGGS.
Orange lustre, one with the painted inscription ''John Hailes''. Decorated with painted floral patterns within oval panels.

Probably Ball's Deptford Pottery, c. 1870, length 2¼in. (5.7cm).

Sunderland Museum Collection.

22. JUG.
Decorated with an east view of the Monkwearmouth Railway Bridge, transfer-printed in purple. The Wear Bridge, as rebuilt 1858-59 is shown behind. The railway bridge, designed by T. E. Harrison, Chief Engineer of the North Eastern Railway, was opened in 1879 and enabled the railway from Newcastle, which hitherto had terminated at Monkwearmouth Station, to be extended across the River Wear into Sunderland itself.

The railway bridge is still in use. This photograph taken c. 1980 from the south bank of the River Wear shows the east side of the bridge, with the reconstructed Wear Bridge, opened 1929, behind.

Probably Ball's Deptford Pottery, c. 1879, ht. 4¼in. (11.4cm).

Sunderland Museum Collection.

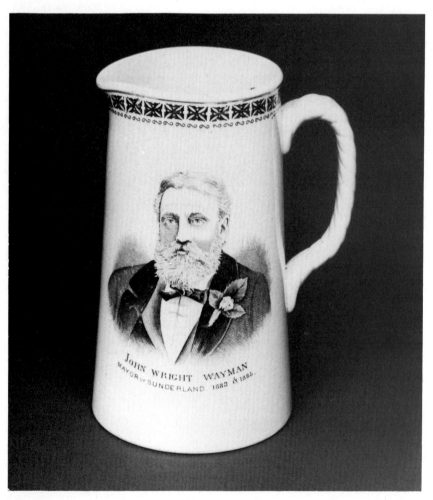

23. JUG.
Decorated with portrait of John Wright Wayman, Mayor of Sunderland in 1883 and 1884, transfer-printed in brown.

Ball's Deptford Pottery, c. 1884, ht. 7⅜in. (18.7cm).

Sunderland Museum Collection.

HIGH SOUTHWICK POTTERY

This pottery was established about 1850 by Thomas Snowball, who was born in Southwick in about 1830 and had been apprenticed at Moore's Wear Pottery as a pot-painter. According to the ground deeds of the pottery (in possession of Alderman Gilbertson of Southwick in 1921) Snowball purchased the land and premises from a Mr. Pratt in 1863. Before this date Snowball probably rented the site (an attached plan indicated a small concern of one kiln and other buildings, sited to the south of the village green). Since Thomas Snowball and his brother, Ralph, worked mainly as pot decorators at their Sheepfolds Warehouse (see p. 48) the management of the pottery, which probably employed only 15 to 20 people, was left in the hands of the foreman, Joseph Thursfield. The pottery proved unsuccessful and according to the *London Gazette* closed in 1885, when the copper plates, moulds, etc., were purchased by Ball Brothers. The site was acquired in 1891 by Alderman Gilbertson who demolished the kiln and buildings.

The pottery does not seem to have marked any of its products and attribution is not easy since output resembled white earthenware and brown ware made by other Wearside potteries. The firm is said to have produced in quantity pink/purple lustre religious plaques (known in the trade as 'scripture tiles'), and examples presented by members of the family are in the Sunderland Museum Collection. The collection also includes a pink lustre mug with the painted inscription 'John Snowball, 1846'. According to the donor, a nephew of John, this piece was made at the High Southwick Pottery by Thomas Snowball himself as a christening present for his son.

PRODUCTS
Brown ware and white ware including religious plaques.

MARKS
No marked examples from this pottery are known.

LOW FORD OR DAWSON'S POTTERY

This pottery at South Hylton, at that time known as Ford, three miles west of Sunderland, was built on land belonging to the Maling family who owned the North Hylton Pottery (see p. 45). The Low Ford Pottery, which fronted the River Wear (Fig. 24), was certainly in existence by 1794 and was well equipped to make 'every species of earthenware'. The pottery had a water mill and other mills for the grinding and preparation of flint and lead[22]. Between 1794 and 1797, when the business was known as 'Sanders and Co.', the pottery was operated by Mr. Andrew Sanders of Bishopwearmouth and others[23]. Their partnership was dissolved on 12th August 1797[24]. The pottery, consisting 'of a kiln for brown ware on a very extensive scale and likewise a kiln for cream coloured ware' was advertised for sale or lease in 1798[25] but by 1799 the pottery was operated by John Dawson who had been trained at the North Hylton Pottery and appears to have been appointed receiver for this works in 1790[26].

---

22 See sale advertisement; *Newcastle Courant,* 4th October, 1794.

23 See notices for sale or lease of the pottery; *Newcastle Courant,* 11th October, 1794, and *Newcastle Courant,* 15th April, 1797.

24 *Newcastle Chronicle,* 4th November, 1797.
    The above are quoted in M.A.V. Gill, 'The Potteries of the Tyne and Wear and their dealings with the Beilby/Bewick Workshop', *Archaeologia Aeliana,* 5th series, vol.IV, 1976, p.160.

25 *Newcastle Chronicle,* 28th April, 1798.

26 See *Newcastle Chronicle,* 9th October, 1790. Notices in the same paper the previous two weeks indicate that the Maling Brothers were in financial difficulties and may have fallen out. This was resolved by the appointment of receivers to carry on the business of the North Hylton Pottery.

John Dawson (1760-1848), married Anna Lakin, and lived in Hylton House. His brother Charles Frederick lived at the Terrace, Hylton. They were the sons of William Dawson of Hunter's Hall, Bishopwearmouth, who had married Elizabeth Laws of Ryton in 1758, receiving from her a substantial dowry. Dawson appears to have worked an extensive business operating a pottery which produced tiles, in addition to brown ware and creamware[27]. He opened a shop and warehouse in Newcastle in 1816[28]. John Dawson's sons, Thomas (1796-1839) and John (1798-1832) helped him run the business[29] which continued to expand.

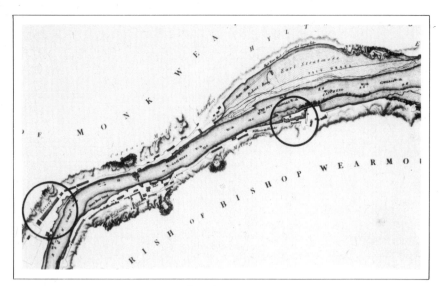

24. Detail of map showing the Low Ford Pottery (right) sited on the south bank of the River Wear, and the North Hylton Pottery (left) further upstream, on the opposite bank. John Rennie's map of the River Wear, scale: 10 inches to 1 mile, 1819-22.

25. MUG.
Creamware, with painted inscription "T. Franklin" and transfer-printed with "An East View of the Iron Bridge erecting over the Wear near Sunderland". (Bridge View 35).

Printed mark: OLDE SANDERS LOW FORD POTTERY.

Sanders' Low Ford Pottery, c. 1793-96, ht. (approx.) 6in. (15.2cm).

Private collection.

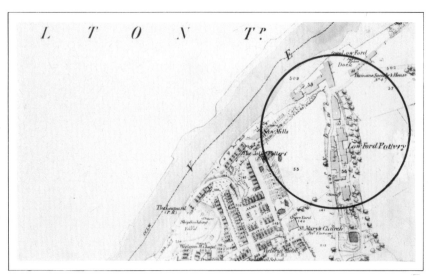

26. Detail of map showing the original Low Ford Pottery buildings sited by the River Wear and pottery buildings erected in the dene to the south by John Dawson in 1836. Ordnance Survey Map, scale: 25 inches to 1 mile, 1857 edition. Durham Sheet VII, 16.

27   "To be sold . . . All that valuable and complete Freehold Estate of Land, situate at Hilton Ferry . . . now in the several Occupations of John Dawson and Co. . . . and others, as Tenants thereof. Also, all those Tile-Sheds, Tile-kiln, and a Kiln for burning of Fire-Bricks . . . Also, one Moiety, of Half-Part, of all that extensive Pottery, called Hilton Low Ford Pottery, with a Water-Mill adjoining, and now let to Messrs. John Dawson and Co. . . ." *Newcastle Courant,* 2nd August, 1801.

28   John Dawson & Co., Hylton Low Ford Pottery . . . have opened a Shop and Warehouse in Newcastle, at the Folly Wharf, East End of the Quayside, which they will keep regularly supplied with such an Assortment of Earthenware, as they trust will give Satisfaction . . ." *Newcastle Courant,* 14th December, 1816.

29   According to an indenture dated 1837, in the Sunderland Museum Collection, the firm was known as Thomas Dawson and Co.

In 1836 new buildings were erected in the dene which ran down to the River Wear (Fig. 26). The foundation stone was laid by Andrew White, M.P., first Mayor of Sunderland, whose sister had married Thomas Dawson. New machinery was installed and with these improvements and good supplies of Devon clay the pottery was reputed to be the best on Wearside, producing good quality earthenware and having the largest output in the area. The pottery employed large numbers in the first half of the 19th century.

When John Dawson died in 1848 at the age of 88, his sons having predeceased him, this flourishing concern fell into the hands of untrained trustees of his grandsons, John and Charles Frederick. Both later took over the management, but, according to local legend, failed to agree and each set up separate businesses. John is said to have operated the main pottery producing white earthenware whilst Charles is supposed to have made brown ware at Bank Top, South Hylton, this probably being the brick and tile kilns advertised as early as 1801[30]. Neither proved successful and the plant, including moulds and copper plates for transfer-printing were sold by public auction in 1864. It is likely that the main pottery closed in that year, although the firm 'John Dawson and Co. Earthenware Manufacturers' still occurs in the Directory for 1867-8, as being at Low Ford.

The considerable amount of glass slag found on the site of Dawson's Pottery, in an excavation carried out by the Friends of Sunderland Museums, indicates the furnaces were subsequently used for bottle-making. According to Christie's Directory of 1871 the premises were operated by Cuthbert Marr as the South Hylton Bottle Co. On 13th August, 1871, the buildings adjoining the furnaces, used for the storage of bottles were damaged in a serious fire[31] and it is unlikely the bottle works was re-opened. Certainly the premises were derelict by 1877 (Figs. 27 and 28), and the 1895 Ordnance Map shows the site vacant, as it still is today.

Also listed in the 1867-8 Directory is 'John Inman, brown earthenware manufacturer, South Hylton'. It is possible he took over the Bank Top Pottery from Charles Frederick Dawson. Moreover, according to Directories of 1873 and 1879 William Ball of the Deptford Pottery was in business at South Hylton listed as 'earthenware manufacturer and brickmaker', implying he operated the Bank Top Pottery for a short time. According to an advertisement in the *Pottery Gazette,* 2nd January, 1882, Ball's also sold ground flint and this suggests the flint crushing mill formerly operated by Dawson's was still in use.

27. Low Ford Pottery, 1877.
Photograph, showing the derelict kilns of the original part of the pottery. The 'Bank Top' tile and brick works can be seen to the left.

28. Low Ford Pottery, 1877.
In this photograph, the chimney of the extensions erected in 1836 can be seen in the background, just to the left of the derelict kilns.

30 *Newcastle Courant,* 2nd August, 1801.
31 *Sunderland Times,* 15th August, 1871, p.2.

29. TOBACCO HOLDER.
Creamware, painted with overglaze enamel floral patterns and verses.

Impressed mark: DAWSON.
Dawson's Low Ford Pottery, dated 1839, ht. (approx.) 3in. (7.6cm).

Private Collection.

30. JUG.
Creamware, with banding in black enamel and decorated with transfer-print of 'The Battle of the Nile' (Admiral Nelson's victory over the French Fleet, 1798) and the design 'May Peace and Plenty'.

Printed mark: DAWSON & CO., LOW FORD.
Dawson's Low Ford Pottery, c. 1800, ht. 8in. (20.3cm).

Sunderland Museum Collection.

31. PUNCH POT.
Creamware, painted with inscription, floral pattern and banding in black enamel and transfer-printed with a landscape design and ''An East View of the Wear Bridge'' (Bridge View 20), signed ''Edward Barker''. The floral pattern on the lid is transfer-printed.

Probably Dawson's Low Ford Pottery, c. 1800, ht 8½in. (21.6cm).

Sunderland Museum Collection.

32. VEGETABLE DISH.
With pierced rim and transfer-printed with romantic landscape design in blue.

Impressed mark: DAWSON.
Dawson's Low Ford Pottery, c. 1840, length 10¼in. (26cm).

Sunderland Museum Collection.

33. PLATE.
Creamware, with banding at rim in brown enamel and transfer-printed with oriental landscape design, overpainted with enamel colours.

Impressed mark: DAWSON.
Dawson's Low Ford Pottery, c. 1800-10, dia. 10¼in. (26cm).

Private Collection.

34. PLATE.
Decorated with classical landscape design showing the pyramid of Caius Cestius, Rome, transfer-printed in blue.

Impressed mark: DAWSON.
Dawson's Low Ford Pottery, c. 1820-40, dia. 8¼in. (21cm).

Sunderland Museum Collection.

35. FIGURE OF A BULL.
Decorated in brown lustre.

Impressed mark: indistinct.
Probably Dawson's Low Ford Pottery, c. 1840, ht. 8¾in. (22.2cm).
Sunderland Museum Collection.

36. CHRISTENING EGGS.
Transfer-printed with designs in purple. One egg has the painted inscription ''Jane Clow'', the other ''John Clow''.

Probably Dawson's Low Ford Pottery, c. 1850, length 2¼in. (5.7cm).
Sunderland Museum Collection.

37. JUG.
Decorated with banding in purple lustre and transfer-printed with floral patterns and the design 'Napoleon', overpainted with enamel colours. ''George and Eleanor Hodgson, 1841'' is painted in purple lustre below the spout.

Printed mark: NAPOLEON, DAWSON. Dawson's Low Ford Pottery, dated 1841, ht. 7½in. (19.1cm).
Sunderland Museum Collection.

PRODUCTS

Dawson's produced the best quality wares on Wearside in many varieties and included creamware with overglaze enamel decoration, transfer-printed creamware (Pl.I, p.2) and yellow-glazed earthenware (Pl.VIII, p.22), transfer-printed tableware in various patterns (Pls.XI, p.26 and XIII, p.27); and pink lustreware, including tea-sets transfer-printed with Adam Buck designs or painted with 'Cottage Lustre' pattern (Pl.XV, p.30). Of special interest are transfer-printed and enamelled pottery eggs (Fig. 36), bachelor supper sets (Pl.XIII, p.27), earthenware 'penkers' (marbles or alleys, either for games or for putting in kettles to prevent furring), wall plaques decorated with hand-coloured transfer-printed landscapes (Pl.XVII, p.31) or the 'Napoleon' battle scene (Fig. 37), and children's money pots, decorated with transfer designs, embellished with overglaze enamel and copper and purple lustre (Fig. 38). Such items have a more 'individual' character and indeed Dawson's are said to have especially encouraged their workmen to produce any novelty which took their fancy. A figure of a bull (Fig. 35) in brown lustre is attributed to the pottery. The firm is also supposed to have produced large busts of Napoleon. These are scarce because the mould from which these were made was stolen before many copies were made. In addition to brown domestic ware the firm produced utility items in white earthenware[32].

MARKS

The Olde Sanders Low Ford Pottery (see Fig. 25 and Bridge View 35). Dawson (impressed); Ford; Ford Pottery, South Hylton, 1800; Dawson & Co., Low Ford; J. Dawson & Co., Low Ford Pottery; J. Dawson, Low Ford (many of these form part of transfer designs). Printed marks such as Dawson or Dawson 'semi-china' are found on tableware, together with the name of the pattern.

32   In an account of Sunderland Polytechnic Society exhibition 15th September, 1838: ''Dr. T.R. Torbock exhibited his invention . . . a vessel for inhalation (earthenware, manufactured by Thomas Dawson, Esq , Ford Pottery near Sunderland). . .''

38. MONEY POT.
Decorated with banding and the figure of a lion cub painted in copper lustre and transfer-printed designs of children, overpainted with enamel colours.

Probably Dawson's Low Ford Pottery, c. 1850, ht. 4¾in. (12.1cm).
Sunderland Museum Collection.

NEWBOTTLE POTTERIES

Newbottle has a special interest for collectors of Sunderland pottery as the Austin, Moore, Scott and Dixon families all lived there (or elsewhere in the parish of Houghton-le-Spring) before leaving to found their own celebrated potteries on the banks of the River Wear. Most of them were trained at the firm of Byers and Co., Newbottle. The Jolly Potters Inn, which still exists in Newbottle, happily recalls the once famous industry.

A pottery known as the 'High' is believed to have been founded in Newbottle about 1720, with kilns in Pottery Yard behind Dial House, for the manufacture of common brown ware for local use. Flint crushing mills were established there in 1740, after which the manufacture of white ware began. In 1766, the 'High' belonged to Byers and Co., a well-known Houghton family whose name occurs repeatedly in the church records. William Byers died in 1758, and Thomas in 1785[33]. Byers would appear to have been succeeded in or before 1777 (for which year and the following one Sunderland Museum possesses the Petty Cash Accounts) by the Scott family of Houghton. Anthony Scott appears as manager in 1788, but in that year he and his father, Henry, went into business at Southwick, the Newbottle concern being taken over by Robert Fairbairns, who ran it for a considerable period. Some time between 1841 and 1851 the pottery was acquired by John Brodrick, at first in partnership with James Beckwith, who appears in the 1841 Census as 'journeyman potter, 35, of Monkwearmouth'. In the 1851 Census Beckwith is listed as 'Earthenware manufacturer, 46, firm of two, employing 22 men, 13 women, 11 boys'. In the same Census Brodrick is given an identical description with his son William, aged 21, shown as 'earthenware printer'. In Directories of 1856 and 1858 Beckwith appears as 'Gentleman' and 'Private Resident' respectively. There seems little doubt that a partnership existed between Beckwith and Brodrick and that the former later withdrew. Brodrick continued to operate the pottery, acccording to Jewitt's *Ceramic Art*, manufacturing chiefly brown ware and flower pots, closing down prior to 1878. In 1890 Mr. Embleton of Sheepfolds, Monkwearmouth, Sunderland saw the broken kilns and ruins of the works in Pottery Yard, since built over.

The other pottery in Newbottle, known as the 'Low' was occupied successively by Ralph Watson up to 1728[34], a Mr. Wilson up to 1765[35], and later by George Harle who is given in the 1841 Census as 'potter' and in that of 1851 as 'earthenware manufacturer, 36, born Portsea, Hants.' Harle is known to have operated a small pottery for making brown ware, known as the 'New Pottery', from 1850, his name appearing in the Directories up to 1873. It is not known whether the 'New' was a different pottery from the 'Low'. The name 'Pottery Yard' in Houghton-le-Spring itself suggests that a pottery was worked there, and indeed, three barrows of 'spoil' were dug up from here during road-widening operations in 1968.

The 1851 Census return mentions yet another potter, of whom nothing so far is known. He is described as 'James Barlow, 33, Earthenware Manufacturer, born Burslem'. There is no mention of him in any of the local Directories of the time.

PRODUCTS
Few authenticated examples of Newbottle pottery are known. Sunderland Museum has a teapot (Fig. 39) with painted green and red floral

39. TEAPOT.
With floral decoration in relief painted in enamels.

Probably Brodrick's 'High' Pottery, Newbottle, c. 1851, ht. 6½ in. (16.5cm)
Sunderland Museum Collection.

40. CREAM JUG.
Transfer-printed with 'Tea Party' design and verse with painted surround in purple enamel.

Probably Brodrick's 'High' Pottery, Newbottle, c. 1860-75, ht. 3in. (7.6cm).
Sunderland Museum Collection.

LADIES ALL
PRAY MAKE FREE
AND TELL ME HOW
YOU LIKE YOUR TEA

---

33   For a pedigree of the family, see R. Surtees, *The History and Antiquities of the County Palatine of Durham,* vol.I, 1816, p.180.

34   Houghton Church Registers record the death on 10th August, 1728, of Ralph Watson, Newbottle Tile Kilns.

35   ''To be let and entered upon immediately at Newbottle, in the County of Durham. The pottery which for many years was carried on to great advantage by the late Mr. Wilson, well fitted with all conveniences and workmen. Also a large stock of clay, flint and other materials for making both white and brown ware, which are now made to as great perfection as in Staffordshire. Enquire of Mr. Mowberry or Mr. Thomas Cook at Bishopwearmouth.'' *Newcastle Chronicle,* 25th May, 1765.

decorations in relief presented by the late James Corder, and said by the original owners to have been made at Brodrick's Pottery in 1851. A small transfer-printed plate and a book of recipes for pottery glaze mixtures used by the Fairbairns were both given by Mr. W. H. Fairbairns, grandson of Robert, owner of the 'High' Pottery. A small cream jug (Fig. 40) transfer-printed in red and green with design of a tea-party and verse, "Ladies all I pray make free," was said by the donor, a native of Newbottle, to have been made there. The Victoria and Albert Museum have in their collections the following examples given by Mr. W.H. Fairbairns in 1905: Vase, with lid, decorated with painted design of trees and cottages in pink lustre; circular plaque with religious motto, "Praise ye the Lord", and broad band of copper lustre on rim; glazed, moulded earthenware figure of a goat; a bust of John Wesley; a child's plate with daisy-pattern embossed rim and central transfer of a girl holding a bird; a set of three children's plates with embossed rims with mottoes, each with a differing transfer design and verse and with the general title, 'Flowers that Never Fade' (Fig. 42). The attribution of this wide range of pottery to Newbottle has been questioned despite the fact that the donor was a descendant of the owners of the 'High' Pottery and presumably had knowledge of its products. The children's plates in particular would normally be regarded as Staffordshire products, yet a sherd of a wasted plate (Fig. 41) uncovered from Newbottle in 1980[36] showing a fragment of 'Flowers that Never Fade' is evidence that such pottery was, in fact, made in Newbottle and probably at other Wearside potteries.

The late Mr. Vernon Ritson, a Sunderland collector, had a pair of lions with well-authenticated pedigree, said to have been made at Newbottle, while a former potter of Brodrick's told Corder that he made pottery lions when employed there. The late Capt. George Earl, a well-known local collector, alleged that coffee pots in the form of a man riding on the back of a goose were also produced and he himself had specimens in both brown and coloured white ware.

A further product said to be of Newbottle origin is the 'Polka' jug, which has on one side, in relief, the figures of two dancers and on the other an embossment with tracings in cobalt blue. The Polka came into vogue about 1841.

MARKS
No marked examples from the Newbottle potteries are known.

41. SHERD (of a wasted child's plate).
The fragments, excavated from Newbottle in 1980, show part of a transfer-printed design from the series entitled, 'Flowers that never Fade'. The fragments reveal the plate was unsuccessfully fired during the glazing stage.
Probably Fairbairns' 'High' Pottery, Newbottle, c. 1830-40, length 5⅜in. (13.7cm).
Sunderland Museum Collection.

42. CHILD'S PLATE.
Decorated with the design 'Politeness', transfer-printed in red. This is one in a series of scenes entitled 'Flowers that never Fade' which illustrate Benjamin Franklin's 'Morals', 'Proverbs' and 'Maxims'. The rim is decorated with lettering in relief.
Probably Fairbairns' 'High' Pottery, Newbottle, c. 1830-40, dia. 6in. (15.2cm).
Victoria & Albert Museum Collection, on loan to Sunderland Museum.

36   This was the most interesting 'find' from a dig undertaken by the staff and Friends of Sunderland Museums and residents of Newbottle on the supposed spoil tip of the 'High' Pottery, but the small number of fragments of white and brown earthenware which were uncovered indicated that the actual site had not been successfully located.

NORTH HYLTON POTTERY (HYLTON POT WORKS)

This pottery was established in 1762 by William Maling of Hendon Lodge, Sunderland, owner of estates at Ford and North Hylton, three miles west of Sunderland, as a business interest for his two sons, Christopher Thompson (1741-1810) and John Maling (1746-1823). The pottery had a river frontage for the shipment of goods and was sited near good beds of natural clay (Fig. 24).

The Maling family, originally Huguenot refugees, had settled in Scarborough in the 17th century. William Maling came to Sunderland in 1723 and in 1740 married Catherine, daughter of Christopher Thompson of Hendon Lodge, Sunderland, which he inherited through his wife in 1749, living there until his death in 1765. He acquired lands after the death of his father in 1743 from whom he inherited a considerable fortune. The North Hylton lands were part of the Hylton Castle Estate. Christopher Thomas Maling was educated at Cambridge for the bar and lived at various times at Hendon Lodge, Silksworth House and Herrington Hall. John Maling became a partner in the Sunderland Banking House of Russell, Allan and Maling and built and lived in the Grange, Bishopwearmouth. Because neither had training in the pottery industry and because both were young when the Hylton Pottery was established the management of the business, initially at least, seems to have been placed in the hands of others. The Beilby/Bewick Workshop supplied the Hylton Pottery with copper plates for transfer-printing to a 'Mr. Turnbull' in 1774 and a 'Mr. Burrell' from 1776 and 1778[37], indicating these two men were probably employed by the Maling Family to operate the pottery. By 1780 the name of the firm is given as Phillips and Maling with a Mr. John Phillips acting as manager, but there is no record of a partnership[38].

In or about 1797 John Maling's son, Robert (1781-1863) joined the business. In July 1815 he transferred the business to a completely new works, the Ouseburn Bridge Pottery on Tyneside which was operational two years later. In 1853 the works passed into the hands of Robert's son, Christopher Thomas Maling (the second of this name) who in 1859 established the Ford Pottery in Ford Street, Ouseburn, Newcastle (in the same year the old Ouseburn Bridge Pottery was sold to Bell Brothers who re-opened the premises as the Albion Pottery). In 1879 C.T. Maling opened the huge New Ford Pottery at Walker, Newcastle calling it the (B) Factory to distinguish it from the Old Ford Pottery known as the (A) Factory. The latter closed during the General Strike in 1926 and the New Ford Pottery closed in 1963[39]. These factories should not be confused with the Low Ford Pottery (commonly known as Dawson's) which was established in the late 18th century on land belonging to the Malings on the south bank of the River Wear in an area known as Ford, now called South Hylton.

After the Malings had transferred their business to Tyneside in 1815, the North Hylton Pottery was taken over by John Phillips, or his son. Phillips already owned the Sunderland ('Garrison') Pottery. After its amalgamation with the larger concern in Sunderland, the North Hylton Pottery produced similar articles and probably copper plates for transfer-printing were exchanged between the two works. The North Hylton Pottery continued as a small-scale concern; in the 1841 Census there were only 26 people living in North Hylton engaged in the pottery industry. The pottery must have closed before 1851 because in the Census of that year it is described as ''The whole of an earthenware manufactory, unoccupied and going rapidly to decay''. The returns show only three potters living in North Hylton and presumably these worked at Dawson's Pottery on the south bank of the River Wear.

37 M.A.V. Gill, 'The Potteries of Tyne and Wear and their dealings with the Beilby/Bewick Workshop'. *Archaeologia Aeliana*, 5th series, vol.IV, 1976, pp.156, 167.

38 A notice in the *Newcastle Chronicle*, 25th September, 1790, does not mention Phillips: ''All persons indebted to the Proprietors, Messrs. Christopher and John Maling. . .''

39 For further information on the Maling business on Tyneside see R.C. Bell, *Tyneside Potteries*, 1971, and R.C. Bell, L. Dixon and S. Cottle, *Maling, A Tyneside Pottery*, Tyne and Wear County Council Museums, 1981.

PRODUCTS

Copper plates supplied by the Beilby/Bewick Workshop in the last three decades of the 18th century indicate that the pottery produced creamware tea and dinner services printed in a variety of designs including animal, floral and landscape patterns. In the late 18th and early 19th centuries the pottery produced typical Sunderland creamware mugs and jugs transfer-printed with masonic emblems, Wear Bridge views and designs connected with seafaring such as 'Jack on a Cruise'. Creamware christening and marriage mugs with painted lettering and sometimes verses, with overglaze enamel floral designs in reddish/brown, yellow and green seem to have been a speciality of the firm (Pl.VI, p.19). Other products of the pottery consisted of pink and copper lustreware and common brown ware.

After the closure of the North Hylton Pottery its transfers were used at the 'Garrison' Pottery as a jug has been noted with transfer designs incorporating maker's marks from both potteries.

MARKS

Hylton Pot Works (rare, said to be found on late 18th century creamware mugs); John Phillips, Hylton Pottery; Phillips and Maling (is said to occur, but as yet no examples have been identified).

SEAHAM POTTERY

The Seaham Harbour Pottery was built in 1836 by Captain Plowright of Lynn for the manufacture of brown ware. In 1838 the business was taken over by a group of workers from Dawson's Pottery who converted the works to the production of printed white ware. The concern was operated on a small scale until its closure in 1841. Sunderland Museum has a breakfast cup and saucer printed with 'Forest' pattern in pale blue (Fig. 43) and an oval meat plate printed in blue 'Willow' pattern (Fig. 44). Both are impressed 'John Allason Seaham Pottery' and presumably these examples date to the period 1838-41.

In 1851 the pottery was re-opened under the ownership of R.C. Wilson. There is then some uncertainty about the future history of the business. The pottery may have been demolished in 1852 but Fordyce in his *History of the County of Durham,* 1857, states that ''Seaham Harbour Pottery belongs to Mr. John Hedley Walker''. This is borne out by an entry in the Census return for 1851, which gives 'Pilot Houses. John H. Walker, aged 41, Earthenware Manufacturer, born Monkwearmouth'.

PRODUCTS

Brown ware and transfer-printed tableware.

MARKS

John Allason Seaham Pottery (impressed; rare).

44. MEAT PLATE.
Transfer-printed with 'Willow' pattern in blue.

Impressed mark: JOHN ALLASON, SEAHAM POTTERY.
Allason's Seaham Pottery, 1838-41, length 16⅛in. (41cm).

Sunderland Museum Collection.

43. BREAKFAST CUP AND SAUCER.
Transfer-printed with 'Forest' pattern in pale blue.

Impressed mark: JOHN ALLASON, SEAHAM POTTERY.
Printed mark: FOREST.
Allason's Seaham Pottery, 1838-41, dia. (of saucer) 6¾in. (17.2cm).

Sunderland Museum Collection.

SHEEPFOLDS OR RICKABY'S POTTERY

This pottery was established in 1840 at Sheepfolds on land lying south-west of the present Monkwearmouth Railway Station Museum (Figs. 45 and 46). The owner, Thomas Rickaby, was born in Newbottle about 1795 and may have worked in one of the potteries there before moving to Monkwearmouth about 1833. At first the business was operated on a small scale with one kiln and in 1851 employed three women and five men, including the owner's son Thomas J. Rickaby (b. 1833) who was apprenticed to his father. Later the pottery was extended when two larger kilns were built.

In 1847 the firm was known as Rickaby and Blakelock and appears as such in the 1850 Directory. Subsequently it was listed as Rickaby and Co. (Ward's Directory 1857) and four years later as Executors of T. Rickaby (Rickaby's widow appears to be carrying on the business since in the 1861 Census she is described as 'earthenware manufacturer'). By 1865 the firm had become T.J. Rickaby and Co.

In December 1900, after T.J. Rickaby's death the business was transferred to Snowdon and Co., of the Bridge Pottery (see p.29).

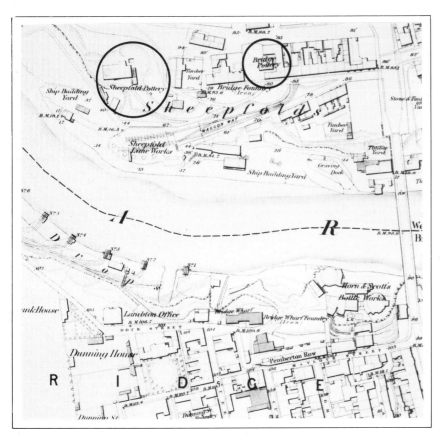

46. Photograph, 1884, showing Sheepfolds Pottery, on the north bank of the River Wear.

45. Detail of map showing Sheepfolds Pottery (left) and the Bridge ('Jericho') Pottery (right).
Ordnance Survey Map, scale: 25 inches to 1 mile, 1857 edition. Durham Sheet VIII, 14.

PRODUCTS

Output comprised mainly brown domestic ware including salt kits (to be hung beside the fire to keep the salt dry). The business was in no way connected with the Sunderland ('Garrison') Pottery but orders for brown ware accepted by this firm were passed on to Rickaby's Pottery for execution, indicating that the 'Garrison' concentrated on the production of white ware in its later history.

It is likely that Rickaby's Pottery also produced white earthenware; a bachelor's supper set (Pl.X, p.23) is attributed to the firm.

MARKS

No marked examples from this pottery are known.

SHEEPFOLDS WAREHOUSE

These premises at Sheepfolds, Monkwearmouth, operated by Thomas Snowball, owner of the High Southwick Pottery (see p.37) were not a pottery as such, but were used for decorating locally-made white earthenware and sometimes pottery and porcelain brought in from Staffordshire. It is not known when the warehouse was established but it is listed under Snowball in a 1857 Directory.

Initially the warehouse, which had an enamelling kiln, was used to finish off ware (which had already been printed) with lustre and gold decoration. Later much of the ware was completely undecorated, some of it from the nearby St. Bede's Pottery (see p.60) and was printed and decorated by John Snowball assisted by his brother Ralph (b. 1832) who had also trained at Moore's Wear Pottery as a pot-painter. Ralph, who worked for his brother for 35 to 40 years is said to have been the last potter on the Wear who could practise the by then old-fashioned mottled pink/purple lustre style of decoration.

As a sideline the firm enamelled glass rolling pins. These are said to have been retailed at sixpence (2.5p) each and found a ready sale with sailors visiting Sunderland.

The last Directory entry for these premises was in 1885 indicating that the warehouse probably closed in that year together with Snowball's other interests, the High Southwick Pottery and St. Bede's Pottery, Monkwearmouth, acquired in 1883.

MARKS

T. Snowball, Bridge End, Monkwearmouth, Sunderland (printed; on plate in Sunderland Museum Collection).

SILKSWORTH POTTERY

In the mid-18th century a pottery was in existence at Silksworth, three miles south-west of Sunderland. 'Robert Markland, of Silksworth, potter' is mentioned in a trust deed of 1749. There was certainly a pottery at Silksworth before 1754[40]. Local tradition maintains its site was on or near that of the village school. The burial of two sons of 'William Tyrer, potter, of Silksworth', in 1758 and 1759 is recorded in Bishopwearmouth parish registers[41]. Christopher T. Maling (d. 1810), of the North Hylton Pottery lived for several years in Silksworth House, where he maintained a small kiln for experimental purposes.

PRODUCTS

It is assumed this pottery made common brown ware for local use.

---

40   ''To be let at Silksworth near Sunderland, a Pot House. Enquire of Mrs. Ettrick at Sunderland''. *Newcastle Journal,* 12th January, 1754.

41   Bishopwearmouth registers also give: '(marriage) April 29th, 1749 — Daniel Maitland [sic] to Elizabeth Punshon, Silksworth; (burials) July 16th, 1750 — Will, son of Daniel Martland [sic] potter, Silksworth; January 31st, 1722 — John Martland [sic] Silksworth; May 15th, 1738 — George Martland [sic] Silksworth'. It would seem likely that these are all spelling variations of the same name.

SOUTHWICK OR SCOTT'S POTTERY

On 13th June, 1788, Anthony Scott (1764-1847), who had managed Byers and Co.'s pottery at Newbottle, established a new pottery in partnership with his father, Henry Scott and Edward Atkinson of Low Street, Sunderland. The pottery was conveniently sited on the north bank of the River Wear at Southwick, at that time a small township on the outskirts of Sunderland (Figs. 47 and 48). Each partner had a one third share and each contributed the sum of £150 to the project, securing land for a term of 63 years at an annual rent of £25. Apparently it took six months to build the pottery.

Initially the business was known as 'Atkinson and Co.' and operated on a small scale (a payroll for August 1789 shows 27 employees at sums varying from two shillings (10p) to three pence (1p) a day and includes Edward Atkinson's son, Edward Jnr.). In June 1799 the title of the pottery was changed to Anthony Scott and Co.[42]. On the 12th August 1800 Atkinson dissolved his partnership with Scott's by mutual consent[43] and took over a china and earthenware business in Sunderland.

When Henry Scott died in 1829, the firm became known as Scott and Sons, Anthony admitting into partnership his sons Henry (1799-1854) and Anthony (1802-1882). Later, two more sons, William (b. 1816) and Thomas Pearson (1800-1864) worked in the business, though they never became partners. Anthony Snr. retired in 1841, when the concern became known as Scott Brothers and Co. After Henry Jnr.'s death his brother Anthony succeeded to the business as sole proprietor but the firm still traded as Scott Brothers and Co. His son, Anthony (1847-1897), third of the name, became a partner in 1872, the name of the firm being again changed to Anthony Scott and Son as from 31st December, 1872[44]. In 1878, Anthony second retired, leaving his son, Anthony third, as sole owner.

47. Scott's Pottery (left) and Robert Thompson's Southwick Shipyard on the north bank of the River Wear.
Detail of oil painting by D. F. McLea, copied from a photograph c. 1860.
Sunderland Museum Collection.

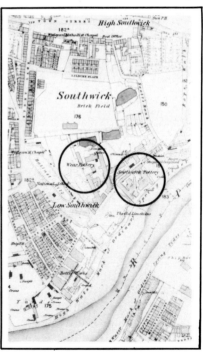

48. Detail of map showing Scott's Southwick Pottery, (right) on the north bank of the Wear and, adjoining, Moore's Wear Pottery, set back from the river.
Ordnance Survey Map, scale: 25 inches to 1 mile, 1857 edition. Durham Sheet VIII, 10.

42   This is indicated in the firm's ledger for that date.

43   *London Gazette,* 12th August, 1800.

44   This is evident from a letter dated 1872, in the Scott papers in the Sunderland Museum Collection.

49. A range of brown ware items made at Scott's Pottery.
Studio photograph, c. 1880, taken by Stabler and Fries of Sunderland.

By this time the pottery had grown considerably and employed about 150 people. Its produce was varied and often of high quality and there was an extensive home trade supplemented by considerable exports to the Continent. However, from a perusal of correspondence with Scott's continental customers during the latter part of the 1870s, it is evident that things were amiss. There is constant complaint of non-arrival of goods, breakages, delivery of 'seconds', accusations that cheaper prices were being quoted by Staffordshire potters and repeated requests for a wider range of new designs. Customers found particularly infuriating Scott's practice of packing smaller common, undecorated articles (which carried a lower import duty), inside larger, decorated items, charged at a higher rate. Duty payable at the higher rate for decorated ware was then automatically charged on all items, thereby reducing the dealer's profits.

In 1888 the pottery celebrated its centenary, and shortly after the works were reconstructed with the most modern machinery. Trade, however, declined. From the firm's ledgers it is evident that the concern was operating at a loss from about 1892: a note added in red ink in Anthony Scott's hand at the end of the year includes: ''. . . The finest flower of this pottery is faded. . .'' The pottery was closed from July to December, 1893[45], and worked half-time during 1894. The firm finally closed down in 1896, a few months after Anthony fourth had joined it on leaving school. His father was taken ill and died in the following year. The last entry in the shipping books for goods ex-warehouse stock was made in November, 1897. The plant, etc., was sold by auction on 26th November of the same year, some of the copper transfer plates being bought by Ball Brothers and later used at their Deptford Pottery.

45 *Sunderland Weekly Echo,* 14th July, 1893.

PRODUCTS

Throughout its long history the pottery produced brown ware[46]. Its range of domestic ware included slip-decorated baking trays and fireproof oven dishes (Fig. 49).

The earliest dated piece of local pottery in the Sunderland Museum Collection is a heavy creamware rice dish, incised on the back 'A.S. 1789' (Fig. 51). It was presented to the Museum by the Scott family in 1879 and it is thought that it was initialled by Anthony Scott to commemorate the start of production at the Southwick Pottery, which, allowing time for construction, would have occurred early in 1789. The pottery must have produced a variety of creamware in the late 18th century and early 19th century but marked examples are unknown. Creamware mugs marked 'Atkinson & Co.' are said to occur. The transfer-print of the Wear Bridge (view no. 2; see p.75) has 'E.A.' incorporated within the bottom of the design. These initials are probably those of the engraver of the copper plate from which the transfer was taken but it is possible they stand for Edward Atkinson.

51. RICE DISH.
Creamware, inscribed on base, ''A. S. 1789''. This is the earliest dated example of Sunderland pottery in the Sunderland Museum Collection and was probably made by Anthony Scott to celebrate the opening of the Southwick Pottery, which, allowing time for its construction, probably took place in 1789.

Scott's Southwick Pottery, dated 1789, dia. 13in. (33cm).

Sunderland Museum Collection.

50. BOWL.
Purple lustre, decorated with transfer-print of the 'Great Eastern', overpainted in enamel colours. 'The Great Eastern' was designed by Isambard Kingdom Brunel (1806-1859) as a cargo and passenger ship capable of carrying sufficient coal for a non-stop voyage to Australia. She was provided with various forms of power: two paddle engines, two screw engines and eight masts. At the time of her launching in 1858 she was the largest ship in the world — 692ft. long and displacing 18,914 tons. Her size was not exceeded for 40 years.
The ship became ''the most ambitious failure in steamship history''. She entered service on the New York route but she was never filled to capacity and made a constant loss. In 1864 she was sold and for the next ten years was used for cable-laying; she laid the first successful transatlantic telegraph cable. This new role was briefly interrupted in 1867 when she made a voyage from Liverpool to New York to attract passengers to the Paris Exhibition. After years of being 'laid up' the ''Great Eastern'' was scrapped in 1889.

Impressed mark: SCOTT.
Scott's Southwick Pottery, c. 1860, dia. 9⅛in. (23.2cm).

Sunderland Museum Collection.

52. BOWL.
Purple lustre, decorated with various transfer-prints overpainted in enamels, including a design of 'April'.

Probably Scott's Southwick Pottery, c. 1840, dia. 8¼in. (21cm).

Sunderland Museum Collection.

46   ''Wanted against Martinmas, two good Brown Ware Firemen, to work either by Day or by the Piece. Enquire of Anthony Scott, Southwick Pottery. . .'' *Newcastle Courant,* 12th October, 1811.

53. Left: JUG.
Pink lustre, with floral transfer-prints overpainted in enamel colours, on handle and inside and outside of rim (a decorative characteristic of Scott's pottery) and transfer-printed verses and design of 'A Sailor's Farewell'. Compare this version with Fig. 6, p.16 and Pl. VII, p.22.
Scott's Southwick Pottery, c. 1840-50 ht. 5¾in. (14.6cm).
Sunderland Museum Collection.

Right: MUG.
Pink lustre, transfer-printed with 'The Sailor's Return' design, overpainted in enamel colours.
Probably Scott's Southwick Pottery, c. 1830-40, ht. 5in. (12.7cm).
Sunderland Museum Collection.

54. JUG.
Pink lustre, transfer-printed with floral patterns, on handle and inside and outside of rim, and various designs including a version of 'The Farmer's Arms', overpainted in enamel colours.
Probably Scott's Southwick Pottery, c. 1830-40, ht. 8¼in. (21cm).
Sunderland Museum Collection.

55. JUG.
Purple lustre, transfer-printed with floral patterns on handle and inside of rim, overpainted in enamel colours, and portrait of John Wesley.
Probably Scott's Southwick Pottery, c. 1830-40, ht. 4½in. (11.4cm).
Sunderland Museum Collection.

56. EWER.
Purple lustre, transfer-printed with floral patterns inside and outside of spout and overpainted "Crimea" design, showing the flags of Great Britain and France, allies against Russia in the Crimean War, 1854-5.
Probably Scott's Southwick Pottery, c. 1855-60, ht. 8¼in. (21cm).
Sunderland Museum Collection.

57. Background: FRUIT DISHES.
Brown earthenware, transfer-printed in yellow slip with 'Lattice Work' pattern (left) and 'Basket Weave' or 'Plaited Cane' pattern (right).

Impressed mark: SCOTT BROTHERS.
Scott's Southwick Pottery, c. 1850, length 12½in. (31.7cm).

Sunderland Museum Collection.

Foreground: TILES.
Brown earthenware, transfer-printed in yellow slip with 'Mosaic' pattern (left) and 'Paisley' pattern (right).

Scott's Southwick Pottery, c. 1850, width 4¾in. (12.1cm).

Sunderland Museum Collection.

58. Items from a TOY COFFEE AND TEA SET.
Painted with repeat stylized floral pattern in overglaze enamels.

Impressed mark (plate): SCOTT.
Scott's Southwick Pottery, c. 1860-80, ht. (of coffee pot) 5½in. (14cm).

Sunderland Museum Collection.

59. CHRISTENING JUG.
With spout in the form of a face-mask and copper lustre banding at rim. Painted with design of a potted plant in copper lustre and overglaze enamels in brown, green and blue. The painted lettering is in black enamel.

Probably Scott's Southwick Pottery, dated 1830, ht. 7¾in. (19.7cm).

Sunderland Museum Collection.

The pottery produced the usual range of pink lustre mugs, jugs and bowls, decorated with transfer-printed designs, verses and views of the Wear Bridge in its original and rebuilt form, the latter also appearing on orange lustre examples. A decorative feature associated with Scott's products is the use of floral transfers, in black, applied outside and inside the rims of jugs, ewers and mugs (Figs. 53, 54 and 55). The 'Crimea' transfer (Fig. 56) was a popular design but was used by other potteries, and indeed the transfers used by Scott's were frequently the same as those used by the nearby Wear (Moore's) Pottery. Moreover, according to the firm's records Scott's supplied earthenware to Moore's Wear Pottery and to the Bridge End Pottery, presumably plain for decoration. Scott's also purchased ware from both Maling and Fell of Newcastle.

Interesting items produced by Scott's are the brown ware dishes and coffee pots decorated with yellow transfer-printed designs such as 'Paisley' and 'Basket Weave' patterns (Pl.V, p.19 and Fig. 57). Thomas Pearson Scott is said to have invented this process which probably involved the use of yellow slip and not ink in the application of the pattern. He is supposed to have carried out printing in secret in a separate room. If this is true then all pieces so decorated must be dated prior to 1864, the year in which he died.

60. MEAT PLATE.
Transfer-printed with 'Jeddo' pattern in turquoise.

Impressed mark: SCOTT.
Scott's Southwick Pottery, c. 1860-97, length 16⅝in. (42.2cm).
Sunderland Museum Collection.

61. Left: DISH.
Transfer-printed with 'Vase' design in purple.

Printed mark: VASE.
Scott's Southwick Pottery, c. 1860-97, dia. 5⅞in. (15cm).
Sunderland Museum Collection.

Right: DISH.
Transfer-printed with 'Statue' design in dark blue.

Printed mark: STATUE, S. B. & CO.
Scott's Southwick Pottery, c. 1860-97, dia. 5⅞in. (15cm).
Sunderland Museum Collection.

Most of the output of the pottery consisted of tableware, occasionally left plain, sometimes painted with overglaze enamel decoration (Pl.X, p.23), but mainly transfer-printed. Scott's used an extensive range of patterns (see Appendix III).One of the copper plates for the popular 'Haddon Hall' transfer used on dinner services is in the Sunderland Museum Collection (Fig. 4). The design was usually printed in a purplish-grey colour, known in the pottery as 'mulberry'.

MARKS

Ed. Atkinson; Scott's Superior Fireproof; Scott & Sons, Southwick (as part of transfer design).

Scott (usually impressed); Scott Brothers, S.B. & Co., Scott Warranted Fireproof (impressed).

The following table may help in dating marked examples of Scott pottery, as, although some stamps may have been kept in use after a change of partnership, none showing a change of name could have been in use before these dates:

	Title of Firm	*Marks*
1788-1800	Atkinson and Co.	Atkinson & Co.; Ed. Atkinson (rare).
1800-1829	A. Scott and Co.	
1829-1841	A. Scott and Sons.	
1841-1872	Scott Brothers and Co.	S.B. & Co. (printed); Scott; Scott Brothers (impressed).
1873-1882	A. Scott and Son.	Scott (impressed); S. & S.; A. Scott & Son (printed).
1882-1897	A. Scott.	Scott (impressed).

62. MEAT PLATE.
Transfer-printed with 'Hawthorn' pattern in grey.

Impressed mark: SCOTT.
Scott's Southwick Pottery, c. 1860-97, length 16⅝in. (42.2cm).
Sunderland Museum Collection.

SOUTHWICK UNION POTTERY, LATER THE WEAR OR MOORE'S POTTERY

The Southwick Union Pottery was advertised in the *Newcastle Courant,* 9th February, 1805:

"To be Sold or Let, For the remaining Part of the Lease, of which Thirty-Seven Years are yet unexpired, All those new, large, and commodious Buildings, situated at Low Southwick, and known by the Name of the Union Pottery, being at present used as a Manufactory of Earthen Ware; also a large Stock of Clay, Crate Rods, Moulds, Wheels, Laths and other Utensils fit for carrying on that Trade. These Buildings are extremely well adapted for an extensive Manufactory of Earthen Ware, or may be easily converted into a Glass Work, or other Manufactories, are well situated for shipping Goods, being near the River Wear, where Vessels of considerable Burthen may load or discharge Cargoes, and are one Mile from the Town of Sunderland. For Particulars, apply . . . to Mr. Thos. Brunton, Southwick. . ."

The pottery had been advertised for lease in March, 1802[47] and in May of that year required two foremen for a brown ware pottery[48].

63. MUG.
Creamware, with banding at rim in black enamel, decorated with a transfer-print of a ship being launched with the caption "Britannia Rules the Waves", a reference to British naval victories against the French.

Printed mark: UNION POTTERY.
Brunton's Southwick Union Pottery, c. 1800, ht. (approx.) 6in. (15.2cm).

Willett Collection, Brighton Museum.

Photograph courtesy of The Royal Pavilion, Art Gallery and Museums, Brighton.

64. MUG.
Creamware, with banding at rim in black enamel, transfer-printed with design of 'Susan's Farewell', overpainted in enamel colours.

Printed mark: UNION POTTERY.
Brunton's Southwick Union Pottery, c. 1800, ht. 5¾in. (14.6cm).

Sunderland Museum Collection.

47 "Building to be Let by Contract,
The Building of a Pottery, at Low Southwick, situate near the River Wear, one mile from Sunderland. A plan may be seen by applying to Mr. Brunton, at Southwick; or Mr. Kirkup, Monkwearmouth, where proposals will be received on Wednesday and Thursday next." *Newcastle Courant,* 20th March, 1802.

48 *Newcastle Advertiser,* 15th May, 1802.

According to W.R. Ball[49] the pottery (which he identified by its later name of the Wear Pottery) was established in 1789 by John Brunton (died 1808) in premises adjacent to Scott's Southwick Pottery (Fig. 48). A pottery existed at Southwick as early as 1753[50], and it is almost certain Brunton's Pottery occupied the same premises. The Bruntons were an old and prominent Southwick family who possessed limekilns and were coal fitters. John Brunton's elder brother, Thomas (d. 1782) was the father of Thomas Brunton (1771-1837) who advertised the Southwick Union Pottery in 1805.

In 1805 or at some time later Samuel Moore (1775-1844) and Peter Austin (1770-1863) took over the business in partnership, changing its name to the Wear Pottery and operating under the name of 'S. Moore & Co.' This title remained throughout the history of the pottery, despite changed ownerships. Both Moore and Austin had trained at Newbottle under Robert Fairbairns, and Austin had married Moore's sister, Jane. Neither stayed in the business for long and by 1831 Moore's son, Charles (1779-1852) was managing the concern. Nevertheless, in the 1841 Census Samuel Moore is listed as 'Earthenware Manufacturer, High Street, Southwick'. By 1826 Austin had established himself as a shipbuilder, a business still carried on in Sunderland as Austin and Pickersgill.

Trade grew steadily and a branch, known as the Bridge or 'Jericho' Pottery (p.29) was opened in 1844 for the production of brown ware. By 1847 Charles Moore had been joined in partnership by his nephew George Storey Moore (b. 1824) who, on his uncle's death, became sole proprietor and operated the business until 1861. In that year the pottery, under a mortgage, fell into the hands of a Sunderland solicitor R.T Wilkinson. Determined to restore its fortune he appointed Ralph Seddon from Staffordshire as manager and on his advice the works were largely rebuilt and equipped with modern machinery. From 1866 to 1872 the pottery was said to be the largest on Wearside, employing 180 hands, and enjoying a good home and export trade, chiefly to Denmark and Germany.

In 1874, Seddon left to set up his own business — the St. Bede's Pottery on Richmond Street, Monkwearmouth (see p.60). After 1875 the Wear Pottery was leased, with the 'Jericho' branch to Messrs. Glaholm, Robson and Lyall, who were plumbers and ironfounders, Lyall being the active partner. They placed it under the management of John Patterson, probably of the family which operated the Sherriff Hill Pottery, Gateshead. The firm then concentrated chiefly on making dinner sets of various patterns, abandoning what it considered the old-fashioned transfer-printed pink lustreware. The venture was not a success and the pottery closed down in 1882, being sold to Robert Thompson, shipbuilder, whose premises it adjoined, for £4,000 'for four acres of land, buildings, machinery — everything very cheap'[51]. It was demolished by 1883.

PRODUCTS

In addition to brown ware the Southwick Union Pottery produced creamware. Transfer-printed mugs marked 'Union Pottery' are extremely rare (Figs. 63 and 64). A Bridge View incorporating the mark 'J. Brunton' is said to occur but no examples are known.

Moore's Wear Pottery produced a full range of articles including brown ware, decorative flower pots (Fig. 66), plaques with coloured transfer designs, copper, silver and pink/purple lustre. The latter included mugs, jugs and bowls transfer-printed with Wear Bridge Views, as well as designs and verses connected with seafaring, religion and politics. Often the transfers were identical with those used by Scott's Southwick Pottery. Many jugs, mugs and bowls have (instead of the usual pink/purple lustre decoration), the rims and bottoms edged with red, green or blue, and zig-

65. VASE.
With 'dragon' handles painted in purple enamel, transfer-printed with wood-grain effect in grey.

Impressed mark: MOORE & CO.
Moore's Wear Pottery, c. 1860, ht. 12¾in. (32.4cm).

Sunderland Museum Collection.

66. FLOWER POT AND STAND.
With banding at rims in crimson enamel and relief decoration overpainted in enamel colours.

Impressed mark: MOORE & CO.
Moore's Wear Pottery, c. 1870, ht. 6¼in. (15.9cm).

Sunderland Museum Collection.

67. WALL PLAQUE.
The borders decorated with stencilled design in blue and transfer-printed with 'Waverley' design.

Printed mark: WAVERLEY, S. MOORE & CO., SUNDERLAND.
Moore's Wear Pottery, c. 1840, ht. 8¾in. (22.2cm).

Sunderland Museum Collection.

49 W.R. Ball, 'Potteries of Sunderland and Neighbourhood', *Antiquities of Sunderland,* vol.VII, 1906, pp.38, 42.

50 ''To be now lett, situate at Southic, near Sunderland, a good new house for making pots and earthenware, now built near the River Wear. Enquire of Mr. Thomas Hall at Southic.'' *Newcastle Journal,* 27th January, 1753.

51 Entry in red ink in Scott's ledger.

68. PLATE.
With pierced rim and broad band painted in green enamel with a design of a bird catching a beetle painted in purple lustre.

Impressed mark: MOORE & CO.
Moore's Wear Pottery, c. 1820-30, dia. 8¼in. (21cm).

Sunderland Museum Collection.

69. BOWL.
Purple lustre, transfer-printed with 'Hunting' designs, overpainted in enamel colours.

Impressed mark: MOORE & CO.
Moore's Wear Pottery, c. 1840, dia. 11½in. (29.2cm).

Private Collection.

70. BOWL.
Pink lustre, transfer-printed with various designs and mottoes from 'Aesop's Fables', overpainted in enamel colours. The base has a printed diamond mark indicating that these designs were registered at the Patent Office Design Registry on 24th December, 1853.

Impressed mark: MOORE & CO.
Printed mark: AESOP, S. MOORE & CO.
Moore's Wear Pottery, c. 1854-60, dia. 11¼in. (28.6cm).

Sunderland Museum Collection.

71. LADLE, TUREEN AND STAND.
Transfer-printed with 'Excelsior' pattern in blue.

Impressed mark (stand): MOORE & CO.
Printed mark (stand): EXCELSIOR, S. M. & CO.
Moore's Wear Pottery, c. 1860-82, ht. (of tureen) 11¾in. (29.8cm).

Sunderland Museum Collection.

zag patterns in the same colours painted in the spaces between transfers (Pl.XVIII, p.31). This decorative treatment seems to have been especially popular at the Wear Pottery although it was also used at Dawson's Pottery. Moore's produced a great deal of tableware transfer-printed with designs including 'Asiatic Pheasants'; 'Clyde'; 'Etruscan'; 'Excelsior' (Fig. 71); 'Key Border' (Fig. 73); 'Tournament'; 'Waverley'; 'Wild Rose' and 'Willow' patterns. Plates, plaques and teapots transfer-printed with a series of eight designs called 'The Bottle' (Figs. 72 and 121) were based on engravings by George Cruickshank (1792-1878), the caricaturist, who produced these in 1847 in aid of the Temperance Movement. Complete sets of plates (which the Stockton Pottery also produced) are rare.

MARKS
J. Brunton (is said to occur incorporated in Bridge View transfer but as yet no examples have been identified).
Union Pottery (incorporated in transfer designs; rare).
Moore & Co., Stoneware, Southwick; Moore & Co. (impressed); Samuel Moore & Co., Sunderland; Moore & Co., Southwick (printed); S. Moore & Co.; S.M. & Co. (impressed and printed, in the latter form usually occurring with the name of the transfer pattern).

73. PLATE.
Transfer-printed with 'Key Border' pattern in brown.

Impressed mark: MOORE & CO.
Printed mark: KEY BORDER, S. M. & CO.
Moore's Wear Pottery, c. 1860-82, dia. 9½in. (24.1cm).

Sunderland Museum Collection.

72. TEAPOT.
Decorated with transfer-printed patterns on handle, lid, rim and foot-ring and scenes V to VIII from 'The Bottle', a series of eight designs based on engravings by George Cruickshank (1792-1878). These were produced in 1847 in aid of the Temperance Movement and show the declining fortunes of a family which took to drink.

Printed mark: THE BOTTLE, S. M. & CO.
Moore's Wear Pottery, c. 1850-60, ht. 10in. (25.4cm).

Sunderland Museum Collection.

ST. BEDE'S POTTERY, MONKWEARMOUTH

Ralph Seddon, who had managed Moore's Wear Pottery (see p.57) for
R.T. Wilkinson, built this pottery in Richmond Street, Monkwearmouth, in
1874. It was a small concern of two kilns which made common white ware
mainly for the London market, but it also produced and supplied frog-mugs
and the like to Thomas Snowball's Sheepfold's Warehouse (see p.48) for
decoration. Seddon died before 1883, in which year the Directory gives the
firm as Francis and Henry Seddon, trading as Seddon Brothers, St. Bede's
Pottery. The business did not prosper and Snowball took it over for a short
while. When he went out of business in 1885, the pottery was closed and
dismantled.

PRODUCTS
Items in Sunderland Museum reputed to have been made at this pottery
include an inkstand, vase and spill-holder in coloured glazes (Pl.II, p.18), a
white earthenware tobacco jar and a marbled-pattern ewer.

MARKS
This pottery does not seen to have marked its products.

74.   Mouth of the River Wear, showing the Sunderland ('Garrison') Pottery (foreground, right) sited on the south bank with the
town barracks, from which the pottery took its name, and the South Dock behind.

Detail from a 'View of an improved entrance to Sunderland Harbour', designed 1849 by Thomas Meik. Drawn and lithographed by M. &
M. W. Lambert of Newcastle.

Sunderland Museum Collection.

SUNDERLAND OR 'GARRISON' POTTERY

The Sunderland Pottery was situated at the east end of the town fronting the River Wear near its mouth and was called the 'Garrison' because of its close proximity to the town Barracks erected in 1794 (Fig. 74). Probably the pottery was established prior to 1753 although there is no absolute certainty that the 19th century business occupied the same site as the premises advertised in that year[52].

According to the Sunderland Rate Book for 1799-1800 a house, wharf and kiln was in the ownership of John Thornhill and Co. who in 1807 leased the premises to John Phillips[53], who was already involved in the operation of Maling's North Hylton Pottery (see p.45). The Beilby/Bewick Workshop accounts reveal that in 1810 several copper plates for transfer-printing (including the 'Tythe Pig' and 'Aerial Balloon'; see Pl.VIII, p.22 and Fig. 75) were supplied to John Phillips and Co., Sunderland Pottery, Thornhill's Wharf, Sunderland[54].

It is likely that Robert Dixon (1779-1844) became a principal partner in the Sunderland Pottery in 1813. Creamware mugs and jugs bear the printed mark 'J. Phillips & Co., Sunderland, 1813' and 'Dixon & Co., 1813', the date referring to the partnership and not to the year of manufacture of the piece. Dixon came from the Newbottle district and lived at North Hylton, where in early life he worked at the pottery. He had three sons, the two youngest, Thomas (1810-1872) and Robert (1816-1856) later becoming partners in the Sunderland Pottery.

In 1815, after the Malings had moved their business to Tyneside, Phillips acquired the North Hylton Pottery which from this time until its closure in the 1840s was operated as a joint concern with the Sunderland Pottery.

On John Phillips' death in 1820, it is likely that William Austin (1778-1852) joined Dixon as principal partner in the business. Austin also hailed from Newbottle. His elder brother Peter was a partner in Moore's Wear Pottery but by 1826 had established himself as a shipbuilder. According to Taylor Potts' *History of Sunderland*, William Austin at one time lived at North Hylton, managing the firm's branch there. His son William (1806-1862) did not become a partner, but worked as a pot-printer, first at Hylton and later as foreman pot-printer at the Sunderland Pottery. His grandson William S. Austin (b. 1833), son of William Jnr., was working as a pot-painter at the 'Garrison' works in 1851.

An indenture of 1825, an agreement of 1827 and an abstract of 1827 (all in the Sunderland Museum Collection) indicate that Thomas Henderson and Alexander Phillips were major partners with Dixon and Austin in the working of the pottery. Little is known of Henderson unless he is the person referred to in a Durham marriage bond of 1792: 'Thomas Henderson, potter Newbottle, and Isa Ransome, Houghton'. Alexander Phillips (1793-1871), son of William Phillips, baker, and presumably nephew of J. Phillips, the elder, acted mainly as a traveller for the Sunderland Pottery at home and on the Continent.

After the death of Robert Dixon in 1844, the business was carried on by his two sons Thomas and Robert with Alexander Phillips. However, the fortunes of the firm steadily declined. The North Hylton Pottery closed in the 1840s and in 1864 the business sold a portion of its land and

75. JUG.
Creamware, with banding in black enamel and transfer-printed with design of "The Ascent of the Aerial Balloon". The reverse is transfer-printed with view 14 of the Wear Bridge.

Printed mark: FROM THE MANUFACTORY OF PHILLIPS & CO.,
SUNDERLAND/PHILLIPS & CO.,
SUNDERLAND, 1813.
Sunderland ('Garrison') Pottery, c. 1813-19, ht. (approx.) 8in. (20.3cm).

Willett Collection, Brighton Museum.

Photograph courtesy of The Royal Pavilion, Art Gallery and Museums, Brighton.

---

52 "To be sold, one or two-thirds of a pot house in Sunderland under a lease of 20 years yet unexpired. It is situate nigh the Pier. Enquire of Mr. Charles Blenkinsop in Durham or Mr. George Blenkinsop in Newcastle." *Newcastle Journal*, 23rd June, 1753.

53 It has been assumed that this John Phillips, who managed the concern and who finally amalgamated it with the North Hylton Pottery, was the son of the J. Phillips who managed Maling's North Hylton Pottery as, by this time, the latter would have reached an advanced age. This may not be the case however, as the name 'Phillips' drops out of the business in 1820 (Piggott's Directory) when presumably Phillips either retired or died. The same directory still lists 'J. Phillips' as at North Hylton, although Dixon and Austin were certainly running both concerns, and this entry is probably in error.

54 Gill, M.A.V.,'The Potteries of Tyne and Wear and their dealings with the Beilby/Bewick Workshop', *Archaeologia Aeliana*, 5th series, vol.IV, 1976, p.163.

mortgaged the balance to its bank as security for overdrafts. In 1865 the partnership was dissolved and the Sunderland Pottery wound up, although its flint crushing mill continued until 1867 in order to fulfil continental contracts for the supply of ground flint. The copper plates for transfer-printing and moulds were purchased by Ball Brothers and used in their Deptford Pottery[55].

77. MUG.
Creamware, with the initials "G.F." and banding at rim painted in black enamel, transfer-printed with 'Farmer's Arms' design, signed "Downing Sct."

Printed mark: DIXON, AUSTIN & CO., SUNDERLAND.
Sunderland ('Garrison') Pottery, c. 1820-26, ht. 4½in. (11.4cm).

Sunderland Museum Collection.

76. Left: MUG.
Creamware, with banding at rim in black enamel, transfer-printed with 'Mariner's Compass' design, signed "Robson Sculpt." Thomas Robson of Sunderland was an engraver of considerable skill and produced several local maps, prints and bookplates, etc.

Printed mark: ENG. FOR PHILLIPS & CO., SUNDERLAND POTTERY.
Sunderland ('Garrison') Pottery, c. 1813-19, ht. 4¾in. (12.1cm).

Sheffield City Museums Collection, on loan to Sunderland Museum.

Right: MUG.
Creamware, with banding at rim in black enamel, transfer-printed with verse and design of a sailing ship, overpainted in enamel colours.

Printed mark: DIXON & CO., SUNDERLAND POTTERY.
Sunderland ('Garrison') Pottery, c. 1813-19, ht. 3½in. (8.9cm).

Sunderland Museum Collection.

55 A copper plate was presented to Sunderland Museum by a member of the Ball family in 1963. The designs 'Sailor's Return', 'The Flag that's braved', and 'The Token', together with the verses 'England, England', 'Now weigh the anchor', 'The sun is up' and 'When tempests mingle' are engraved on a copper plate manufactured by Pontifex and Stiles, 23 Lisle Street, London. In 1834, William Stiles joined Russell Pontifex, up to then trading as R. Pontifex and Son. The name was changed to Pontifex and Stiles until the partnership ended in 1839. As one of the designs on this plate has the name 'Dixon, Phillips & Co', one must assume that the firm changed its name some time between 1834-39. This copper plate appears to have passed into the hands of either Moore's or Scott's (possibly both) and finally to Ball Brothers.

78. JUG.

Creamware, painted in overglaze black enamels commemorating the death and funeral of George IV in 1830 (the King actually died on 26th June, not the 19th as stated on the pot).

The jug was made for "M. Polley, Tolshunt dairey" [sic], but research has failed to trace a person of this name connected with dairying in any of the three villages in Essex called Tolleshunt. However, a *William* Polley (born 1769) of Tolleshunt *d'Arcy*, licensee of the "Queen's Head" in the village, between 1809-16, has been recorded. It is possible the pot-painter misunderstood the information given to him when the commission for this 'one-off' piece was given.

Probably Sunderland ('Garrison') Pottery, c. 1830, ht. 6¾in. (17.1cm).

Sunderland Museum Collection.

79. MUG.

Creamware, transfer-printed with view of the Victoria Railway Bridge at Penshaw. The stone bridge was built to carry the Durham Junction Railway over the River Wear about seven miles upstream from Sunderland. T. E. Harrison supervised its construction. The design of the bridge by Walker and Burges is supposed to have been based on that of the Roman bridge built A.D. 105 at Alcantara in Spain. It was named 'Victoria' because the contractors — Gibb of Aberdeen — completed their work on Coronation Day; June 28th, 1838. Appropriately the mug is also transfer-printed with a crown and portrait of the young Queen Victoria.

Probably Sunderland ('Garrison') Pottery, c.1838, ht. 4¾in. (12cm).

Darlington Museum Collection, on loan to Sunderland Museum.

The Victoria Bridge, shortly after its opening.
Lithograph by G. Hawkins, Jnr., published 1838, by Currie and Bowman, Newcastle, after drawing by J. W. Carmichael.

Sunderland Museum Collection.

Photograph of the Victoria Railway Bridge, taken in 1980.
The bridge is still used today for freight traffic.

80. A group of MASONIC JUGS.

Transfer-printed with various designs, overpainted in enamel colours. The pink lustre example (top left) has a verse beneath its spout painted in black enamel and the three creamware jugs have banding in black enamel.

Printed marks: (jug, above right) DIXON & CO., SUNDERLAND POTTERY; (jug, top left) DIXON & CO., SUNDERLAND; (jug, top right) J. PHILLIPS & CO., SUNDERLAND POTTERY/PHILLIPS & CO., SUNDERLAND POTTERY/PHILLIPS & CO., SUNDERLAND, 1813.
Sunderland ('Garrison') Pottery, c. 1813-19, ht. (jug, top right) 8in. (20.3cm).

Sunderland Museum Collection.

81. SHAVING BOWL.
Copper lustre, with floral patterns painted in enamel colours.
Probably Sunderland ('Garrison') Pottery, c. 1820-30, length 13⅜in. (34cm).
Sunderland Museum Collection.

82. JUG.
Pink lustre, with painted inscription "J. M. W." in black enamel and transfer-printed with design of sailing ships, signed "Downing Sc.". A design of 'The Smith's Arms' is painted in black enamel below the spout. The jug has a capacity of 2½ gallons (11.4 litres) and has an extra handle beneath the spout.
Sunderland ('Garrison') Pottery, c. 1820, ht. 11⅝in. (29.5cm).
Sunderland Museum Collection.

83. Left: WALL PLAQUE.
Purple lustre, with copper lustre border and decorated with a transfer-print of the 'Northumberland 74'. The number relates to the quantity of cannon carried by the warship which conveyed Napoleon to exile on St. Helena in 1815.
Impressed mark; DIXON, PHILLIPS & CO., (surrounding anchor).
Sunderland ('Garrison') Pottery, c. 1815-20, ht. 7¾in. (19.7cm).
Sunderland Museum Collection.

Centre: WALL PLAQUE.
Purple lustre, with copper lustre border and transfer-printed with portrait of Richard Cobden, M.P., the radical politician and publicist. Cobden (1804-65) campaigned for free trade and was a leading figure in the Anti-Corn Law League from 1838. He entered Parliament in 1841 and his efforts contributed to the repeal of the Corn Laws in 1846. He was offered a cabinet post by Palmerston in 1859, but Cobden refused, preferring to remain independent. In 1860 he secured a reduction in trade tariffs between Britain and France.
Probably Sunderland ('Garrison') Pottery, c. 1840-50, ht. 8in. (20.3cm).
Sunderland Museum Collection.

Right: WALL PLAQUE.
Purple lustre, transfer-printed with landscape design.
Impressed mark: DIXON & CO.
Sunderland ('Garrison') Pottery, c. 1820-40, ht. 7¾in. (19.7cm).
Sunderland Museum Collection.

84. TEAPOT.
Purple lustre, with the painted inscription "G. & S. Wrapson" in black enamel and transfer-printed with verse and "Success to the Coal Trade" (with collier-brig, above), the design overpainted in enamel. The lid is painted with a cottage lustre design in enamel colours.
Printed mark: DIXON & CO., SUNDERLAND POTTERY.
Sunderland ('Garrison') Pottery, c. 1820, ht. 5¾in. (14.6cm).
Sunderland Museum Collection.

86. SHAVING MUG.
Purple lustre, with painted inscription ''G. R.'' in black enamel. The lid is transfer-printed with a view of Byland Abbey and an oriental pavillion, overpainted in enamel colours. The mug is transfer-printed with a view of the Wear Bridge and ''The Mariner's Arms'', overpainted in enamel colours.

Printed mark: DIXON & CO., SUNDERLAND POTTERY.
Sunderland ('Garrison') Pottery, c. 1820, ht. 7½in. (19cm).

Private Collection.

87. EWER AND BASIN.
Pink lustre, with copper lustre rims and decorated with various transfer-printed designs.

Impressed mark: DIXON & CO.
Sunderland ('Garrison') Pottery, c. 1830. ht. (of jug) 12in. (30.5cm).

Sunderland Museum Collection.

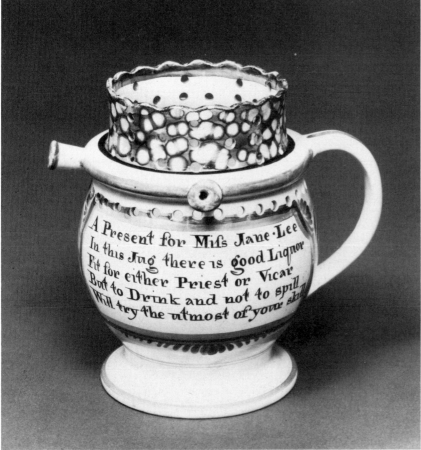

85. PUZZLE JUG.
Purple lustre, (with restored handle), transfer-printed with view of Byland Abbey, over-painted in enamel colours and decorated with hand lettered dedication and verse in black enamel.

Probably Sunderland ('Garrison') Pottery, c. 1820-30 ht. 6in. (15.2cm).

Sunderland Museum Collection.

88. FIGURE OF 'SUMMER'.
Decorated with overglaze enamels.

Impressed mark: DIXON, AUSTIN & CO.
Sunderland ('Garrison') Pottery, c. 1820-26, ht. 9in. (22.8cm).

Sunderland Museum Collection.

PRODUCTS

The Sunderland Pottery had a large home and export trade. It produced yellow-glazed earthenware and creamware (often of high quality) decorated with typical Sunderland transfers, including masonic designs (Fig. 80). It made silver and copper lustreware, an endless variety of pink/purple lustreware including not only the usual jugs, mugs and bowls but also items such as chamber pots, wall plaques and Methodist Love-Feast Cups. The pottery produced impressed figures and watchstands, and sets of the 'Seasons' are known. The firm is said to have produced lions (Fig. 11); statuettes of Joan of Arc, Napoleon, the Duke of Wellington and the Child Samuel; busts of Nelson and John Wesley; shepherd and shepherdess; Highlander with bagpipes and dog, and other figures and chimney-piece dogs. However, such unmarked pieces are difficult to attribute with any certainty since similar examples were made in Staffordshire.

'Garrison' products of special interest are carpet bowls (Fig. 89) and transfer-printed or enamel-decorated pottery eggs. The firm produced tea-sets (including transfer-printed designs based on engravings by Adam Buck), and transfer-printed dinner services for the local market and for export to the Colonies (a romantic landscape pattern used by the 'Garrison' Pottery is called 'Australia'; Pl.XII, p.26) and to the Continent.

MARKS

J. Phillips, Sunderland Pottery; Phillips and Co.; Dixon, Austin & Co., Sunderland; Dixon, Austin, Phillips & Co.; Phillips and Co., Sunderland, 1813; From the manufactory of J. Phillips, Sunderland; Dixon, Austin and Co. (impressed); Dixon and Austin's Sunderland Potery [sic]; Phillips and Co., Sunderland Pottery; Dixon & Co.; Dixon & Co., Sunderland Pottery; Dixon & Co., Sunderland; Dixon, Phillips & Co. (impressed; surrounding an anchor); D.P. & Co. (impressed; square mark); Dixon & Co., Sunderland, 1813.

The following table gives probable dates of ownership of the Sunderland Pottery and will help to date products:

1807-1812	John Phillips
1813-1819	Phillips & Co. and/or Dixon & Co.
1820-1826	Dixon, Austin & Co.
1827-c.1834-39	Dixon, Austin, Phillips & Co.
c.1834-39-1865	Dixon, Phillips & Co.

89. CARPET BALLS.
Decorated with sponged patterns or banding in enamel colours. In conjunction with a smaller, white 'jack' such balls were used in the Victorian indoor game of carpet bowling. Probably Sunderland ('Garrison') Pottery, c. 1830-65, dia. 3in. (7.6cm).
Sunderland Museum Collection.

90. TEAPOT.
Transfer-printed with 'Turkish Pavilion' pattern in brown.
Printed mark: TURKISH PAVILION, DIXON & CO.
Sunderland ('Garrison') Pottery, c. 1830, ht. 5¼in. (13.3cm).
Sunderland Museum Collection.

91. BREAKFAST CUP AND SAUCER.
Transfer-printed with pattern in purple-black.

Impressed mark: DIXON & CO.
Sunderland ('Garrison') Pottery, c. 1840, dia. (of saucer) 6in. (15.2cm).

Private Collection.

92. PLATE.
Transfer-printed with 'Nonpareil' pattern in purple-black.

Impressed mark: DIXON & CO.
Printed mark: NONPAREIL, DIXON PHILLIPS & CO.
Sunderland ('Garrison') Pottery, c. 1840-65, dia. 10½in. (26.7cm).

Sunderland Museum Collection.

SUNDERLAND POTTERY CO., MILLFIELD, LATER THE WEARSIDE POTTERY

The Sunderland Pottery Co. was established in 1913, the directors being Alderman W. Walker, Digby Nelson, Frederick Nelson, H.E. Pitt and A.P. Pitt, who was also the manager. It was built in Alfred Street, Millfield, well planned, with modern machinery and produced a wide range of brown ware from local clay. Yellow and white ware using clay from Wareham, in Dorset, were also made. About 30 hands were employed, most of the older ones having worked at Ball's Deptford Pottery. The trade name of the firm was 'Sunrex'.

In 1927, Alderman Walker died and the company was reconstructed by Messrs. D. and J. Crombie under the name of 'The Wearside Pottery Co.' In the following year electrically-driven machinery was installed and, whilst still making a certain amount of brown ware, the new firm extended its scope, specialising in the manufacture of fireproof ivory-coloured cooking ware and ornamental ware. Examples of the firm's products are in the Sunderland Museum Collection including jugs showing a design in relief of the present Wearmouth Bridge of 1929 (Fig. 94).

The later production of the firm was limited to yellow ware for kitchen use, the most popular item being lined mixing bowls supplied to the home and export markets. At its peak, the firm was employing up to 60 hands; by 1957 the number had dropped to 15. Production ceased in February and the plant and equipment were sold by auction on 20th and 21st March, 1957.

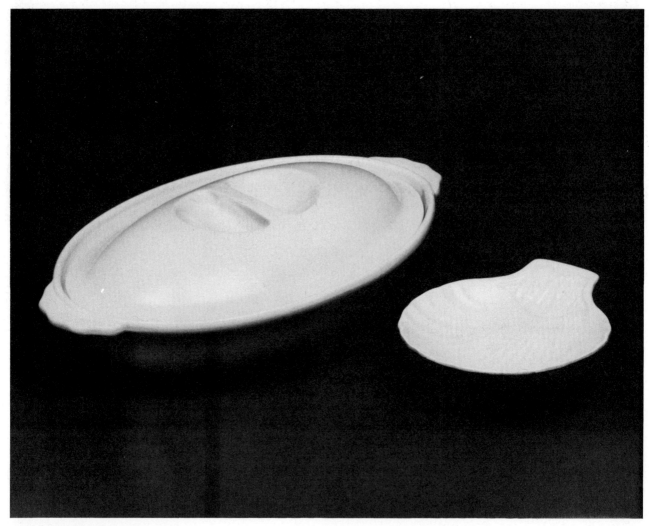

93.   CASSEROLE AND SHELL-DISH.
The former oversprayed with yellow enamel and the base of the latter oversprayed in turquoise enamel.
Wearside Pottery Co., c. 1939, length (of casserole) 11¾in. (29.8cm).
Sunderland Museum Collection.

94. JUG.
With relief decoration of the Wear Bridge, as re-constructed in 1929, and the Sunderland Crest, oversprayed with shaded effect in brown enamel.
Wearside Pottery Co., c. 1930-39, ht. 7¾in. (19.7cm).
Sunderland Museum Collection.

The manager, Mr. R.P. Pitt, then started a pottery, under the same name, at Seaham. The pottery used clay from Derbyshire and Staffordshire and most of the products were sold on a contract basis to china dealers and pet shops. The firm, subsequently operated by B.W. Pitt, son of R.P. Pitt, also produced hand-made 'Craft Pottery' including jugs and coffee sets.

PRODUCTS
Early products made by the Sunderland Pottery Co. were brown coarse-ware and items such as lamp reflectors for street lights, water troughs for poultry and jars for chemicals made from Dorset white clay.

The Wearside Pottery Co. continued to make brown ware but extended its scope, making cooking and ornamental ware including casseroles, mixing bowls, bulb bowls, vases, trinket sets, figures, clock sets and match-holders. Later production was limited to kitchenware. Such items were made at Seaham, supplemented by 'Craft Pottery'.

MARKS
Sunrex; Ovenware (printed and impressed); Wearside Pottery Co., Millfield, Sunderland (impressed).

95. MUG AND JUG.
Reproduction Sunderland purple lustre, the mug transfer-printed with sailing ship design
and the jug transfer-printed with view of the Wear Bridge of 1796. The printed factory
mark can be seen on the base of the mug.

Printed mark: GRAY'S POTTERY, MADE IN STOKE-ON-TRENT, ENGLAND.
A. E. Gray & Co. Ltd. Hanley, c. 1950-60, ht. (of jug) 5⅛in. (13cm).

Sunderland Museum Collection.

96. POWDER BOWL AND PLATE.
Reproduction Sunderland purple lustre, the former transfer-printed with sailing ship and the
latter, transfer-printed with designs of the 'Seasons'.

Staffordshire, c. 1935, dia. (of plate) 9¾in. (24.7cm).

Sunderland Museum Collection.

APPENDIX I
Reproductions of Sunderland Pottery

Collecting Sunderland pottery, especially transfer-printed pink/purple lustreware, has become increasingly popular during the past two decades. Those already collecting or about to start should be extremely wary of buying modern reproductions which are appearing on the antiques market to an ever increasing extent.

The Staffordshire firm of A.E. Gray and Co. Ltd. (established c. 1912), subsequently Portmeirion Potteries Ltd., Stoke, produced white earthenware items such as jugs, mugs, plates and powder bowls decorated with purple lustre and transfer-prints of the Wear Bridge and designs and verses connected with seafaring, which resemble Sunderland products of the 19th century (Figs. 95, 96). Gray's used a factory mark of a sailing ship on most of their products (Fig. 95) but this mark is printed and can be removed. Inexperienced collectors often buy these 20th century reproductions believing them to be 19th century Sunderland pottery. However, the Gray product can be identified by its modern, smooth, machine finish, heavily inked and printed transfers and almost 'too perfect' coatings of purple lustre.

A second category of modern reproduction are those items which have deliberately been made to resemble, in the closest possible way, 19th century Sunderland pottery. These fakes, clearly intended to dupe the unsuspecting buyer, are sometimes extremely difficult to distinguish from the genuine Sunderland article. Many pink lustre jugs, mugs, plates, chamber pots and especially plaques are decorated with transfer designs which are close copies of the original (Fig. 97) or indeed, in rare instances, may have been taken from 19th century copper plates.

Reproduction Sunderland wall plaques are common because they are press-moulded and hence easy to fake; it is more easy to identify reproduction mugs and jugs because these articles do not have the 'throwing rings' which are found on the inside walls of genuine 19th century Sunderland pots. The experienced collector can spot a fake by the appearance of the coating of purple lustre which does not resemble the 19th century product. Moreover, the more he handles genuine pots, the more the collector will be able instinctively to identify a reproduction.

The collector should also note that it is not only pink/purple lustreware which is reproduced. For instance, many modern copies have been made of the frog-mug decorated with applied relief and overglaze enamels showing three old, seated sailors exchanging yarns. Genuine 19th century examples are attributed to the Sunderland ('Garrison') Pottery but many would have been made elsewhere, including Staffordshire.

97. MUG.
Reproduction Sunderland purple lustre, transfer-printed with 'Jack Crawford' design and verse.
Staffordshire, c. 1960, ht. (approx.) 4½in. (11.4cm).
Private Collection.

98. The Wear Bridge of 1796, viewed from the west.
Engraving, published by Reed and Son of Sunderland, dated 1837.

Sunderland Museum Collection.

APPENDIX II
The Wear Bridge

Overleaf are illustrations of the different transfer views of the Wear Bridge found on pottery. Most transfers depict the original bridge, but three Bridge Views (34, 35 and 36) are of the bridge 'to be erected'; 'erecting'; or 'building over the Wear' and consequently date from the period before 24th September, 1793, when the foundation stone was laid, or between this date and 9th August, 1796, when the bridge was opened. Other transfers are of the bridge after it was rebuilt in 1858-59, when, under the supervision of Robert Stephenson, the structure was widened and levelled off.

When a transfer is described as a 'west view' it is the west side of the bridge which is seen, the spectator looking towards the mouth of the River Wear. Where no description is given on the transfer the easiest way of distinguishing between an 'east view' and a 'west view' is to observe the position of the bridge abutment with the large archway. In a 'west view' this appears on the left.

When opened the Wear Bridge was the largest single-span cast-iron bridge in the world and it is not surprising that views of the bridge, printed in black, more rarely in blue or green, and frequently hand-coloured, outnumber all other transfer designs found on Sunderland pottery. The Wearside potters decorated their ware with transfers of the bridge not only because they were proud to commemorate this local landmark but also because they realised that such pottery would make ideal souvenirs, which would be eagerly purchased by local people and the many visitors to Sunderland.

The ingenious idea of bridging the river at Sunderland with a single-span cast-iron bridge was proposed by Rowland Burdon (1756-1838), M.P. for Durham from 1790 to 1806, a leading figure in local commercial circles and an accomplished scholar who had studied architecture under Sir John Soane. The development of Sunderland had been hampered by the town having no bridge. The River Wear could only be crossed by ferries, fords higher up the river and the mediaeval bridge at Chester-le-Street, some miles away. Consequently there was no direct road to Newcastle. Burdon had every incentive for solving the problem of bridging the Wear at Sunderland because he wanted to extend his Stockton-Sunderland Turnpike to Newcastle and South Shields.

The construction of a stone bridge was no answer to the problem because it would require supporting piers which would obstruct river traffic. The bridge which Burdon designed, joining the north and south banks of the Wear with a single span of 236 feet, 100 feet above the low-water mark, was a considerable feat of engineering. The bridge weighed 900 tons, of which 214 tons were of cast-iron and 46 tons of wrought-iron. The bridge had six ribs, spaced five feet apart, each made up of 105 cast iron blocks with a timber superstructure of planking which provided a base for a McAdam-type road. The structure was 32 feet wide with a paved footpath on each side, an iron palisade and lamp posts. The Wear Bridge was an immense advance on the first Iron Bridge at Coalbrookdale, Shropshire, with which it is often confused. The Iron Bridge opened in 1779 had a span of 100 feet, weighed only 376 tons and cost £6,000. The Wear Bridge cost over £32,000 of which Burdon subscribed £30,000.

After its opening in 1796 the Wear Bridge received considerable praise for the method and materials of its construction, its size and elegance. However, as designer of the bridge, and the overseer of its constructor, Thomas Wilson of Sunderland, Burdon has not received the credit he deserves. It is usually claimed, with little justification, that Thomas Paine, the political philosopher, designed the Wear Bridge and that his ideas were copied by Burdon.

Paine proposed bridging the River Schuylkill in Philadelphia by an iron bridge with a 400 feet span. He patented his ideas in 1788. Walkers of Rotherham then made experimental iron bridges of 90 feet and of 110 feet for Paine in 1789. The latter was displayed in London in 1790 after which the structure was broken up and the parts returned to Walkers as scrap. They were not used in the construction of the Wear Bridge but instead remained at Walkers for several decades, some occasionally taken away by curious visitors as mementoes of the author of *The Rights of Man*.

The only connection between Paine's bridge and Burdon's was that Walkers, iron founders of considerable experience, fabricated the iron used in both; otherwise the two structures were quite different. Paine's patent contains vaguely expressed ideas, his bridge comprising ribs of small segments (probably of wrought- and not cast-iron) which fitted together rather like a spider's web. Burdon's ideas expressed in his patent of 1795 and used in the construction of the Wear Bridge were more specific and involved the principle of using cast iron blocks as voussoirs and constructing the span like a stone archway (the spring of the arch of the Wear Bridge was 33 feet)[56].

In 1806 Burdon lost most of his assets in the collapse of a bank in Berwick of which he was a partner. He retired from public life and this, combined with his unassertive nature, probably led to the claims that Paine designed the Wear Bridge. To pay off the debt owed to the bank's creditors the Bridge Commissioners raised the required £30,000 by holding a lottery, the draw for which took place on the 1st December, 1816. Commemorative medals

---

56 For a fuller description of the original Wear Bridge, the contribution of Rowland Burdon to its construction and the bridges of Thomas Paine see S. Miller, 'Burdon in his Iron Boots', *Durham County Local History Society Bulletin,* 18, 1975, pp.41-49 and N. Cossins and B. Trinder, *The Iron Bridge,* 1979, Chap. 7, pp.67-77.

were given to the six thousand subscribers. There were 150 prizes, the highest of £5,000, which were paid off by the bridge tolls. In 1846 the tolls for pedestrians were abolished and other tolls reduced by 50 per cent. At this time a profit of nearly £80,000 had been secured from the bridge but it was not until 1885 that all tolls were abolished.

In the 1850s serious faults developed in the Wear Bridge necessitating its closure in 1858 and its re-construction at a cost of £40,000. It re-opened on the 5th March, 1859. By 1924, owing to increased traffic, this re-built bridge was being seriously overloaded. A new structure was erected (Fig. 100) at a cost of £271,000 without the bridge being completely closed. The new bridge, in appearance very similar to the Tyne Bridge at Newcastle, was opened by King George VI, then Duke of York, on the 31st October, 1929.

99. The Wear Bridge, as re-built 1858-59, viewed from the east.
Engraving, by W. and A. K. Johnston, after the painting by Mark Thompson of Sunderland. Dated 1859.

Sunderland Museum Collection.

100. The Wear Bridge under reconstruction, 1924-29.
Work was carried out without the bridge being closed. This photograph shows the structure of the present Wear Bridge (opened 31st October, 1929) nearing completion.

TRANSFER-PRINTED DESIGNS OF THE WEAR BRIDGE.

The numbering of the bridge view designs follows that of the previous edition. Designs which have been acquired since 1973 have been added to the appropriate group and thus appear out of numerical sequence.

ORIGINAL BRIDGE, 1796 (Fig. 98).

South-East Views:

1. Late 18th/early 19th century.

2. Late 18th/early 19th century. Signed "E. A."; probably the engraver of the copper plate, but the initials may stand for Edward Atkinson, co-owner of the Southwick Pottery 1788-1800.

3. Circa 1820. Marked ''J. Phillips, Hylton Pottery''.

40. Late 18th/early 19th century.

4. Circa 1800. Probably Dawson's Low Ford Pottery.

30. Late 18th/early 19th century.

37. Circa 1820-40.

East Views:

34. 1793-96. Note caption: "of the Bridge *to be erected* across the River Wear near Sunderland".

35. 1793-96. Note caption: "of the Iron Bridge *erecting* Over the Wear near Sunderland". Marked "The Olde Sanders Low Ford Pottery".

36. 1793-96. Note caption: "of the Iron Bridge *Building* Over the Wear near Sunderland".

SUNDERLAND BRIDGE. Built 1793-6. Height 100 feet. Span 236.

5. Circa 1850. Note the paddle steamer in the design.

6. Late 18th/early 19th century.

7. Late 18th/early 19th century.

8. Circa 1820-40. Marked "Moore & Co., Southwick".

20. Circa 1800-20. Signed "Edward Barker".

21. Late 18th/early 19th century.

32. Circa 1820. Probably Dawson's Low Ford Pottery.

33. Circa 1820-40. Marked "Dawson".

9. Circa 1850. Possibly Sunderland ('Garrison') Pottery.

10. Circa 1798-1800. Marked "J. Dawson & Co., Low Ford Pottery". Note the ship beneath the bridge is named "Ld. Duncan". This ship was built by William Havelock (father of General Havelock of Indian Mutiny fame) and launched from his yard in Southwick on 2nd March, 1798. 'Ld. Duncan' was of 925 tons and at that time was the largest ship built on the River Wear.

11. Circa 1810-20. Sunderland ('Garrison') Pottery.

12. Circa 1840-60. Probably engraved for a Tyneside pottery (see Pl. XIV, p.27).

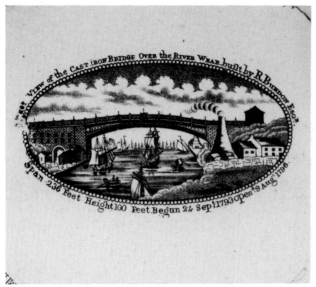

13. Circa 1820-40. Sunderland ('Garrison') Pottery   41. Circa 1820. Marked "Dixon & Co., Sunderland".

14. Circa 1813-20. Frequently marked "Dixon & Co., Sunderland, 1813" or "Phillips & Co., Sunderland, 1813".

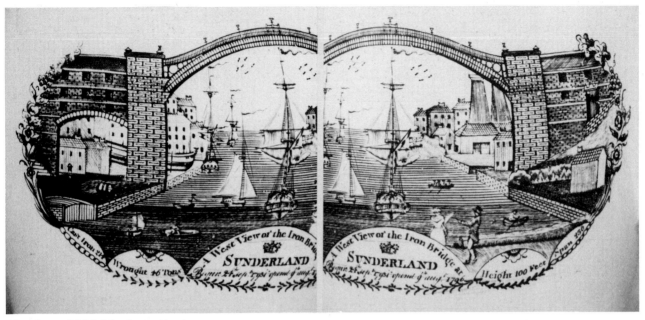

22. Circa 1800-20. Probably Dawson's Low Ford Pottery.

23. Circa 1840-50.

24. Circa 1850. Note the paddle steamer in the design.

25. Circa 1820-40. Marked "Moore & Co., Southwick".

38. Circa 1830-50. Marked "Moore & Co., Southwick".

26. Circa 1820-40.

39. Circa 1850-80. Probably 'Garrison', Moore or Scott, re-used by Ball's Deptford Pottery.

27. Circa 1830. Scott's Southwick Pottery.

28. Late 18th/early 19th century.

st VIEW of the CAST IRON BRIDGE at Sunderland Built by R. BURDON
Span 236 feet Height 100 feet Began 24 Sep. 1793 opend 9 Aug.

29. Circa 1850. Probably Sunderland ('Garrison') Pottery.

31. Circa 1850.

RE-BUILT BRIDGE, 1859 (Fig. 99).

East Views:

NEW BRIDGE OVER THE WEAR AT SUNDERLAND.

15. Circa 1859-70. Scott's Southwick Pottery, Moore's Wear Pottery and probably Ball's Deptford Pottery.

HEIGHT 100 FEET. SUNDERLAND BRIDGE. SPAN 236 FEET.

16. Circa 1870. Probably Ball's Deptford Pottery.

17. Circa 1870. Probably Ball's Deptford Pottery.

18. Circa 1859-70. Scott's Southwick Pottery, Moore's Wear Pottery and probably Ball's Deptford Pottery.

West Views:

19. Circa 1859-70. Scott's Southwick Pottery, Moore's Wear Pottery and probably Ball's Deptford Pottery.

APPENDIX III

Transfer-printed designs used by Scott's Pottery

This alphabetical list of designs used on Scott's tableware, etc, has been compiled from a search of existing account books and in many instances it has been possible to ascertain the earliest date at which designs were used and which firm supplied the copper plates.

In a few instances only the date of repair of a copper plate is known and it must be assumed that in such cases the design had been produced for some time. Because copper is a fairly soft metal the transfer plates were subject to a good deal of wear and required repair. Engraved lines which had become too shallow to hold the required amount of ink were retouched and the plates themselves, which had gradually become curved due to being squeezed between the plate rollers, were flattened out.

In 1970 and 1971 two small 'digs' were organised by Sunderland Museum on the site formerly occupied by Scott's spoil heap. Quantities of decorated, unglazed sherds were discovered, some marked with the pattern name. Now that such patterns have been identified it is hoped that complete examples will come to light.

* Represented in Sunderland Museum by marked specimen.

† Sherd found on Scott's spoil-heap.

Figures shown in brackets indicate the number of plates necessary to decorate the various items comprising the set.

Suffixed numbers in the third column relate to the supplier of the copper plate; see footnotes.

Pattern name	Item	Date copper plate supplied
Albert (2)	Cup and saucer	21 November, 1878[3]
Alphabet (2)		
Alpine (2)	Cup and saucer	26 May, 1875[7]
*† Amoy (4)	Breakfast and tea cup and saucer	1872[7]
† Arabia (2) (Fig. 101)	Cup and saucer	3 October, 1866[6]
Argus		One plate engraved December 1870[3]
Arrow (2)	Tea cup and saucer	31 December, 1877[7]
† Autumn (4) (Fig. 102)	Cup and saucer	1854[8]
Avis (5)		
Balmoral (2) (Fig. 103)		
Bell (2)		
Border (3)	Tea cup and saucer and plate	3 September, 1883[7]
Bosphorus (9)		
Bouquet (1)	Toilet set	5 April, 1865[7]
Broseley (14) (Fig. 104)	Cup and saucer	Before 1854
Butterfly (2)		
Central Exchange	(Ware for hotel)	6 May, 1869[7]
† Chin(4) (Fig. 105)	Breakfast and tea cups and saucers	31 December, 1868[3]
Chuson (3)		
Cock Robin (1)		9 April, 1869[7]
Commercial Hotel	(Ware for hotel)	24 June, 1880
Coral (6)	Breakfast and tea cups and saucers and plates	Prior to 1883 (repairs to plates[3])
Cretonne (1)		
* Crimea (1)	Jugs, mugs, bowls (probably purchased from 'Garrison' Pottery; transfer plate now in Sunderland Museum)	

Denmark (1)		
Doric (1)	Cup and saucer	23 October, 1863[5]
† Dove (2)	Cup and saucer	
* Dresden (1)	Cup and saucer and plate	3 July, 1880[3]
	8 inch plate	21 September, 1884[3]
† Drop (2)	Cup and saucer (breakfast)	9 March, 1864[7]
Eunice (2)	?Cup and saucer	30 September, 1862[7]
Farm (3)	Jugs	12 September, 1883[1]
Farmer's Arms (1)	Bowls, jugs, mugs, etc. Possibly purchased from 'Garrison' Pottery	
Feather (2) (Fig. 106)	Cup and saucer	19 September, 1874[3]
Fern (1)		
Fibre Tea (8)		
Flora (6)		
Florida	Cup, saucer and plate	29 December, 1862[7]
Forest (5)		
† Formosa (26) (Fig. 107)	Dinner Set	
Fruit Girl (6)		
Fuchsia (3) (Fig. 108)	Cup, saucer, plate	14 July, 1862[3]
Garibaldi (1)	Jugs, mugs, bowls, etc. Probably purchased from 'Garrison' Pottery	
Garland (6)	'Twiffler' (pudding plate)	24 August 1861[7]
	Saucer	28 April, 1879[3]
† Gem (6) (Fig. 109)	Breakfast and tea cups and saucers	3 March, 1870[7]
	Size 4 teacup and saucer	30 November, 1875[3]
*† Granite (1)	Cup	
* Haddon Hall (30) (Fig. 4)	Dinner service	1854: plates repaired[8]; plates also repaired[2]; and engraved by[3]
*† Hawthorn (13) (Fig. 62)	Tea cup and saucer	5 April, 1865[7]
	Breakfast cup and saucer	4 May, 1865[7]
	Dinner set	13 June, 1883[1]
Hortulan (7) (Fig. 110)		
Iris (4)	Plate and dishes	June and December, 1881[3]
Ivy (2)		
Japanese Jug (4)		
* Jeddo (5) (Fig. 60)	'Twiffler' (pudding plate)	2 October, 1861[6]
	Dinner set	25 June, 1881[1]
† Lambton Castle (Fig. 111)	Tea plate, saucer, cup, bowl	
† Key Border (13)	Cups and saucers	29 May, 1877[7]
	7 in. and 8 in. plates: 10 in. dish	1884[3]
Ladies All (1)	"Ladies All, I Pray make free And tell me how you like my tea" (?cream jugs)	
Lily (2)		
Marble Sheet (2)	Toilet sets (Ewers, Chambers, Basins, Soap Pots)	
Marble Tea (5)	Plates	12 July, 1870[3]
Marine Views (8)	Cup and saucer	1854[8]
	Breakfast cup and saucer	20 June, 1871[3]
Motto (2)		5 August, 1884[2]; plates repaired[3]
† Nest (3) (Fig. 112)	Jugs	9 April, 1871[7]

Nice	Dinner plate	1869[4]
Number (3)		
Olga (2)	Tea cup and saucer	7 April, 1878[3]
Opaque China (1)	Descriptive label for wares	19 February, 1863[7]
Osborne (15)	Table service	
† Our Early Days (2)	Dinner set	1 June, 1867[7]
	Plate	
Parrot (2)		
Pastoral (6)	Tea cup and saucer	24 March, 1875[3]
	Breakfast cup and saucer	Repaired 1875[3]
† Peacock (7) (Fig. 113)		
† Pearl (2) (Fig. 114)	Cup and saucer	19 August, 1867[6]
Pheasant (17)		
† Pompey	Plate	
Prepare (1)	Scripture tile (plaque)	
Presents (2)		
Priory	Cup and saucer	Plate repaired 1854[8]
Queen's Head Hotel	?Table services	18 July, 1868[7]
Queen's Hotel	?Table services	20 January, 1868[7]
Rhine (6) (Fig. 115)		23 February, 1863[6]
Ribbon (6)	Toilet set	24 March, 1865[6]
Roman	Toilet sets	Mentioned in correspondence 1873
† Rose (6) (Fig. 116)	Cup and saucer	26 July, 1866[7]
Rosenburg (4)	Breakfast and teacups and saucers	15 November, 1879[3]
† Royal Nursery Polka	Plate	
Ruby (4)	Breakfast and teacups and saucers	1870[4]
Rustic (8)		
† Scotch Piper (Fig. 117)	Plate	
Scotch Scenery (5)	Bowls and basins (flanged)	Ordered in 1877, Hamburg
† Seasons (2)	Plate — daisy border: 'February'	
† Seaweed (2) (Fig. 118)	Cup and saucer	Plates repaired 1854[8]
Shield (2)	Cup and saucer	17 September, 1879[3]
Southwick Institute		25 November, 1867[7]
Sportsmen (2)	Teacup and saucer	21 June, 1877[7]
* Statue (Fig. 61)	Saucer	
Stork (6)	4 copper transfer plates	31 January, 1879[1]
	Cup and saucer	5 November, 1879[7]
Swing (2) (Fig. 119)	Cup and saucer	20 March, 1865; plate repaired[2]
Sydenham (2)	Chamber set	26 March, 1861[7]
Thyra (2)	Cup and saucer	25 October, 1878[3]
Thyrasicanthus (4) (spelt several ways)	Toilet set	24 January, 1881[1]
Tonquin (2)		
Tulip (2)	Cup and saucer	25 March, 1878[3]
Tweed (2)	Cup and saucer	10 March, 1862[7]
* Urn (8)	Cup and saucer	15 April, 1865[7]
	Breakfast cup and saucer	6 October, 1865[7]
	Jug, 18 in. and 24 in. plate	19 April, 1875[3]
Vase (1) (Fig. 61)	Saucer	
Vine (2)		
* Willow (28)	Dinner service	Plates repaired 1865[7]

Wreath (16)	Tea plate	Repaired 12 March, 1862[7]
	Dinner service	Before 1877[3]
	New tea pattern	9 April, 1879[3]
† Yew Ting (18) (Fig. 120)		Saucer plate repaired 3 February, 1873[3]

1   BAINES, CHARLES JAMES
He was a china and earthenware merchant in 1851 at Bleak Hill, and later, by 1867, at Wedgwood Chambers, Chapel Square, Burslem.

2   DAVIS, HENRY
16 St. Lawrence, Newcastle upon Tyne.

3   MOWAT, WILLIAM
At 6 Dean Court, Newcastle upon Tyne in 1870.
At 48 Dean Street, Newcastle upon Tyne in 1885.

4   PEPPER, ELISHA AND SON
Elisha Pepper worked for Wedgwood from 1839, and had premises in Slack Lane, Hanley. From 1861-5 he was partner in the engraving firms of Green, Sergeant and Pepper and Green and Pepper. Trading as above, he worked in 1867 from 51 John Street and 40 Vine Street, Hanley.

5   SERGEANT, GEORGE
Had an address in Market Street, Hanley, but by 1867 was listed as at Grove Cottage, Snow Hill, Shelton, Hanley, as an agent for Potters' materials.

6   WILDBLOOD, AMBROSE WOOD
In 1851 at 24 St. John's Square, Burslem, trading as an engraver and clothes dealer. By 1867, his address is given as Queen Street, Burslem.

7   WILDBLOOD, WILLIAM
From 1834-1879 he traded at 44 Navigation Road, Burslem, but by 1889 had moved to 22 King Street, Burslem.

8   WILLIAMS, W.B.
In 1854 he was at 11 Melbourne Street, 11 Derby Street and 33 Melbourne Street, Newcastle upon Tyne. In 1860 he traded from four addresses: 73 Wesley Street, 64 Albert Street, Shieldfield and Alma Row, St. Anthony's, all Newcastle upon Tyne, and from 5 Park Lane, Gateshead on Tyne.

SHERDS (IN THE SUNDERLAND MUSEUM COLLECTION) EXCAVATED FROM THE SITE OF SCOTT'S POTTERY SPOIL HEAP, 1970-71, SHOWING FRAGMENTS OF TRANSFER-PRINTED DESIGNS.

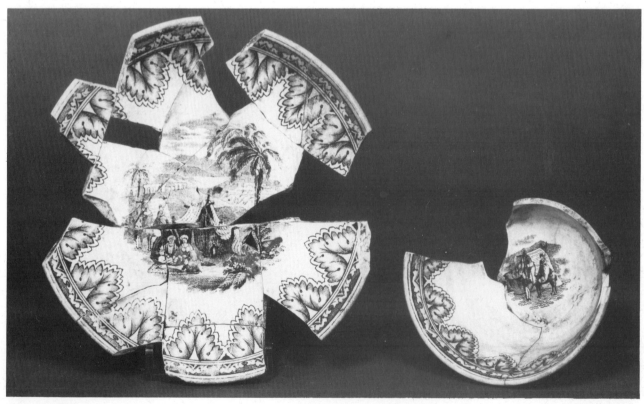

101. 'Arabia'

102. 'Autumn'

103. 'Balmoral'

104. 'Broseley'

105. 'Chin'

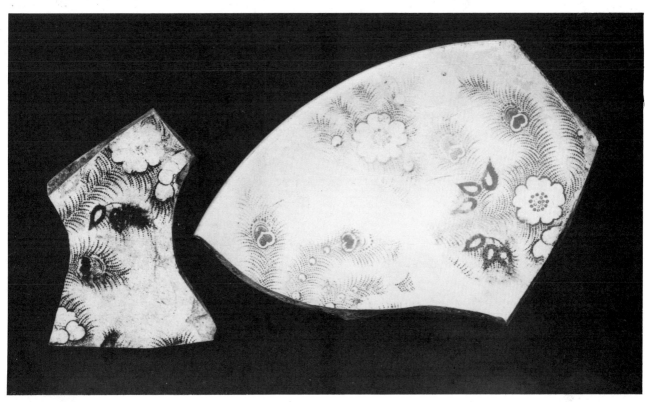

106. 'Feather'

107. 'Formosa'

108. 'Fuchsia'

109. 'Gem'

100

110. 'Hortulan'

111. 'Lambton Castle'

112. 'Nest'

113. 'Peacock'

114. 'Pearl'

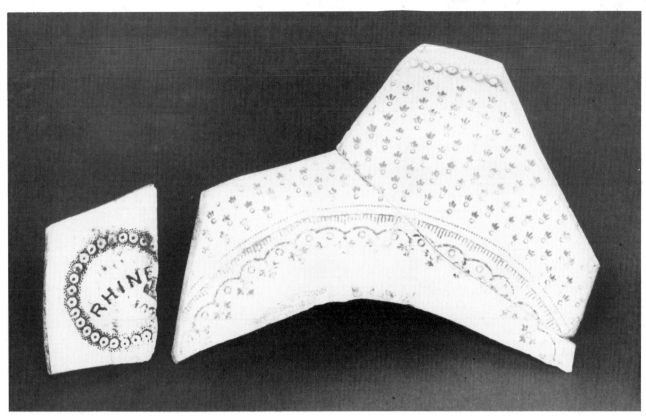

115. 'Rhine'

116. 'Rose'

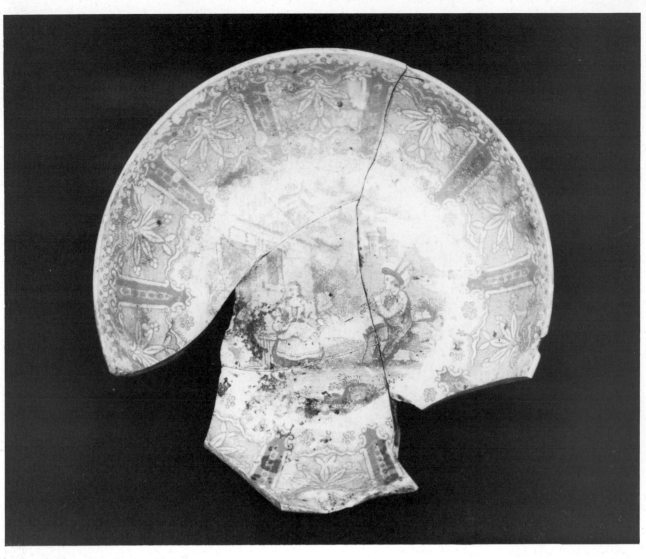

117. 'Scotch Piper'

118. 'Seaweed'

119. 'Swing'

120. 'Yew Ting'

APPENDIX IV
Rhymes, Mottoes and Designs

Most of the entries below are taken from examples in the Sunderland Museum Collection. Others come from publications showing marked pieces, or have been contributed by private collectors for whose information Sunderland Museum is extremely grateful.

The listings are in alphabetical order. Titles, which occur infrequently, are cross-referenced. Entries with a suffixed letter are addenda to the 1973 edition of 'Sunderland Ware'. Wording which actually appears on the item(s) concerned is printed in heavy type.

Variants of designs and verses are included, and original spelling has been retained. Because the copper plates from which the transfers were taken were engraved by different firms all sorts of variations in words, spelling and punctuation occur. Often when transfers were applied to the surface of pots distortion occurred, resulting at times in the disappearance of whole letters.

Much of the creamware and pink/purple lustreware made on Wearside found a ready sale to seafarers and consequently most designs and doggerel verses have a nautical theme. Other subjects covered include local and national personalities and events, religion, Freemasonry, Friendly Societies (Oddfellows, Foresters, Mechanics, etc.), the coal trade, commerce in general, innkeeping and farming. These provide interesting sidelights on the social history of the 19th century.

Designs on tableware manufactured by Scott's Southwick Pottery are listed separately in Appendix III.

1

Adieu, my native land, adieu,
The vessel spreads her swelling sails,
Perhaps I never more may view
Your fertile fields, your flow'ry dales.

Frog-mug.
Ball.

Mug.
Moore.

2

Susan's Farewell
Adieu she cry'd
And waved her Lilly hand

Mug.
Union.

Aesop

(Group of transfer-printed designs and mottoes from 'Aesop's Fables', registered at the Patent Office Design Registry on December 24th, 1853, by Moore's Pottery. See 53A, 118A, 200A, 280A, 309A).

3

The Agamemnon in a storm.

(title below transfer of ship.)

Mug.
Ball.

Jug.
Moore, Scott.

4

Agriculture, the most useful and important
of all pursuits, teaches the nature of soils and
their proper adaptation and management for
the production of food for man and beast.

Jug.
Dawson, 'Garrison', Scott.

5

Ah! Wondrous Me
What do I see?

Chamber Pot.
?Moore or Ball.

6

Alas, how soon this body dies
Its but an earthly clod
Each passing moment loudly cries
Prepare to meet thy God.

Jug.
'Garrison'

6a

Alderman Storey, M.P. for Sunderland.

(title below transfer portrait)

Jug.
Ball.

7

Always speak truth,
But not at all times the whole truth.

Jug.
Ball.

8

Anchor supported either side by sailors.

(transfer design).

Jug.
'Garrison'.

9

Ancient Order of Forresters.

    (title below transfer of coat of arms).

Bowl.
Ball.
Scott.

10

Flowers that never fade
Attention
And when I learn my hymns to say
And work, & read, & spell,
I will not think about my play,
But try to do it well.

Plate.
Newbottle.

11

Anger restrained
Is conquest gained.

Ball.

12

Any Port in a storm, my old Boy — only let us
have lots of grog and a comfortable 'turn in'
and I'll make you Capt. of the fore-top.

Jug.
'Garrison'.

(The Ascent of the Aerial Balloon; see 224).

12a

April

    (title above transfer design on 'months' bowl; see also 199).

Scott.

13

Asiatic Pheasants

    (design on dinner ware).

Moore.

14

As I expect
So let me find
A faithful heart
And constant mind

Jug.
'Garrison'.

15

As I live, saith the Lord
I have no pleasure in
the death of the wicked.

Plaque.
Ball.

(The Ass in the Lion's Skin; see 280a).

16

Jack Crawford, the True British Sailor
At Camperdown we fought,
And when at worst the fray
Our mizzen near the top, boys,
Was fairly shot away.
The foe thought we had struck,
But Jack cried out ''Avast'',
And the colours of Old England
He nailed up to the mast.

Jug, teapot.
Ball.

(**Attention**; see 10).

16a

August

    (title above transfer design on 'months' bowl; see also 199).

Scott.

17

Australian Landscape

    (design on dinner ware).

'Garrison'.

18

Jack on a Cruise
Avast there! Back your maintopsail!

    (motto below a nautical transfer).

Mug.
Phillips, Hylton.

19

Barque

    (title below ship transfer).

Ball.

20
The Battle of the Nile

    (title below transfer of fleet of ships).

Jug.
Dawson.

21

Be familiar with few
Have communion with one
Deal justly with (to) all
Speak evil of none

Jug dated 1831.
'Garrison'.

    (see also 104).

22

Behold! God will not cast away a perfect Man,
Neither will He help the evil doer.
(Job: 8, 20)

Plaque.
'Garrison'.

121. **The eight transfer-printed designs in the series entitled 'The Bottle', shown in detail.**
These examples are from a set of plates impressed "Moore & Co.".
Sunderland Museum Collection.

23

The Best of All   God is with us

   (title above transfer portrait of Wesley; see also 307).

Mug.
Scott.

24

Be such an one in thy life as
Thou wilt wish to be in death

Ball.

25

Better be alone
Than in bad company

Ball.

26

Better to pay and have little left
Than to keep much and be always in debt

Ball.

27

Be wise then, Christian, while you may
For swiftly time is flying
The thoughtless man who laughs to-day
Tomorrow will be dying.

Basin.
Scott.

Bowl.
Ball.

27a

A Blessing

A Blessing on you both I give
Long and happy may you live
May discord never be your lot
But virtue reign within your cot

Chamber Pot.
'Garrison'

27b

Bishopwearmouth Parish Church

   (title below transfer design)

Jug, bowl.
Ball.

28

The Bottle

   (title above eight transfer scenes).

Plate, plaque, teapot.
Moore.

   (George Cruickshank (1792-1878), the caricaturist, produced
   these designs in 1847 in aid of the Temperance Movement. The
   eight scenes, which enjoyed great popularity, depict episodes in
   the life of a family which took to drink).

29

Bouquet

   (design on dinner ware).

'Garrison'

29a

Hugh Bourne.
Born April 3rd, 1772.

   (title below transfer portrait).

Loving Cup.
Ball.

30

La Bretagne — 140 Guns

   (title below transfer of man-of-war).

Jug, basin.
Scott.

31

The Landlord's Caution

The Brewer has sent his clerk
And I must pay my score
So if I trust my beer
What shall I do for more

32

Brig

   (title below ship transfer).

Ball.

32a

Britain's Pride is the Sailor.

Jug.
?'Garrison'

33

Trafalgar

The Britons mourn, what else can Britain do
While bleeding Nelson rises to her view
Still is there cause for triumph when she shews
The captured colours of our vanquished foes.
And greater still when Fame was heard to say
All, all was Nelson's on that glorious day.

Jug.
Phillips, Hylton.

34

Adam Buck designs

   (adaptations of designs by Adam Buck (1759-1833) are found on
   pottery and textiles from c. 1811-1820).

Dawson, 'Garrison'

(Sir Francis Burdett; see 254).

34a

Byland Abbey

    (transfer-printed view).

Puzzle jug, shaving mug.
'Garrison'

35

California

    (design on plate).

Moore.

36

Chantry

    (design on plaque).

Moore.

37

Charity

    (title below transfer of figure).

Bowl.
Moore.

38

Chelmsford Road, 1822

    (pottery design).

'Garrison'

39

China Boquet [sic]

    (design on dinner ware).

Moore.

40

Chintz

    (design on jugs).

Moore.

41

Christ is my pilot wise
My compass is His word
Each storm my soul defies
While I have such a Lord

Jug.
'Garrison'

42

Adam Clarke, LL.D., F.S.A., Wesleyan Minister

    (title below transfer portrait).

Love-Feast Cup.
'Garrison'.
Jug.
Scott.

43

Clyde

    (design on dinner ware).

Moore.

44

Richard Cobden, M.P.

    (title below transfer portrait; see also 92).

    (b. 1804 d.1865. He led the successful campaign to abolish the Corn Laws).

Plaque.
'Garrison'

45

Co-equal with red is the gallant true blue,
And none can its glories o'erwhelm
Whilst Freeman and Sydney direct a brave crew
And William presides at the helm.
Then fill up a bumper, Britannia appears
New-rigg'd and with joy we all hail her;
King William we hail with three times three cheers
And long life to the first British sailor.

Bowl.

46

The Columbus, the largest ship ever built

    (title below ship transfer).

Jug.
Moore or 'Garrison'

47

Come Box the Compass

Plaque.

48

Come my old friend and take a pot
But mark now what I say
While that thou drink'st thy neighbour's health
Drink not thine own away
It but too often is the case while we sit o'er a pot
We kindly wish our friends good health
Our own is quite forgot.

Jug.

49

Cottage

    (hand-painted designs).

Cup, saucer, jug.
Dawson, 'Garrison'

50

Jack Crawford, the Hero of Camperdown

    (title below transfer showing Crawford nailing the colours to the mast. Below, left, **Oct. 17th, 1797** [date of action]; right, **April 7th, 1890** (unveiling of statue in Mowbray Park, Sunderland). Centre, beneath: **Copyright Ball Bros. Sunderland**). This transfer occurs in at least two sizes.)

Jug, teapot.
Ball.

(Jack Crawford, the True British Sailor; see 16).

51

John Crawford

The sailor who so heroically nailed
Admiral Duncan's flag to the main
top gallant mast of the Venerable

(here is shown a reproduction of the Jack Crawford Medal, half-size, which is now in the Sunderland Museum).

after it had been shot away by
Admiral de Winter in the glorious
action off Camperdown Oct. 11th, 1797
Born 1775, died at Sunderland, his
native place in 1831

(Found with this design is a transfer-printed portrait of Jack Crawford nailing the flag, based on the engraving by Daniel Orme (1766-1802) which he made from a sketch drawn on board the flagship *Venerable* and published on 21st November, 1797).

Mug.
Ball.

(Jack Crawford was an early victim of the Cholera plague which swept Sunderland in 1831).

52

Norah Creina Steam Yacht

(title below transfer of ship; Norah Creina, 202 tons, was built in Liverpool in 1825 and sailed between London and Cork).

Bowl.
Moore, Ball.

(Crimea; see 194).

52a

Dear lovely wife pray rise and p-ss
Take you that handle and I'll take this,
Lets use the present which was sent
To make some mirth is only meant,
So let it be as they have said
We'll laugh and p-ss and then to bed.

Chamber Pot.
'Garrison'

52b

December

(title above transfer design on 'months' bowl; see also 199).

Scott.

(Deus Tabit Vela; see 185).

53

Diligently and with reverence
Peruse the Holy Scriptures

Ball.

53a

The horse and the ass.

A disobliging temper carries its own punishment along with it.

Bowl.
Moore.

54

Distress me with those tears no more
One kiss, my girl, and then adieu!
The last boat destined for the shore
Waits, dearest girl, alone for you.
Soon, soon before the light winds borne
Shall I be severed from your sight;
You left the lonely hours to mourne, [sic]
And weep thro' many a stormy night.

('The Sailor's Adieu', by Charles Dibden [1745-1841].

Jugs.
Moore, Ball.

55

Do thy Best
And leave the rest

Ball.

55a

Duke of Wellington — 131 Guns

(title below transfer design).

Plaque.

56

E'en now by faith we join our hands,
With those that went before;
And greet the blood be-sprinkled bands
On the Eternal shore.
Oh that we might now grasp our guide!
Oh that the word were given!
Come, Lord of Hosts, the waves divide,
And land us all in Heaven!

Jug.
Scott.

57

England, England, glorious name
Home of freedom star of fame,
Light o'er ocean widely sent,
Empress of the element.
Gorgeous sea encircled gem,
Of the worlds bright diadem,
Nations, nations to command
Who but points admiring hand
To thee our own our native land.

Bowl.
Scott, Moore, 'Garrison'

58

Etruscan

(design on dinner ware).

Moore.

59

Excelsior

(design on dinner ware).

Moore.

60

Ensigns of state that feed our pride,
Distinctions troublesome and vain,
By masons true are laid aside,
Arts freeborn sons such toys disdain.
Enobled by the name they bear,
Distinguished by the badge they wear.

Bowl.
Moore, Ball, 'Garrison'

61

The Fairy of the Sea

    (title below a ship transfer).

'Garrison'

62

Faithful Watcher

    (design on tableware).

'Garrison'

63

The Sailor's Farewell

Far from home across the sea
To foreign climes I go
Whilst far away O think on (of) me
And I'll remember you.

Bowl.
'Garrison', Scott, Ball.

(**The Farmer;** see 212).

64

Farmer's Arms

    (title below transfer, sometimes with motto; see also 93).

Jug, mug.
Scott, 'Garrison'.

65

Fear not my soul
Be not dismayed
For Jesus Christ
Thy debt has paid

Butter dish.
?'Garrison'

66

February

    (title above transfer design on 'months' bowl; see also 199).

Scott.

67

Feeding Poultry

    (title below transfer design).

Mug.
?'Garrison'

67a

First a Girl, then a Boy.

Chamber Pot.
Ball.

68

First Lifeboat was built
at South Shields

    (title below transfer design of a lifeboat; see also 323).

Ball.

69

The flag that's braved a thousand years
The battle and the breeze.

    ('The Mariners of England' by Thomas Campbell, 1777-1844)

    (motto below transfer design of group of sailors bearing Union Jack).

Jug.
'Garrison', Moore, Scott.

(**Flowers that never Fade;** see 10, 95, 129, 134).

(These are illustrations of Benjamin Franklin's 'Morals' 'Proverbs' and 'Maxims' produced in quantity on mugs and plates during the first half of the 19th century).

70

Forest

    (transfer design).

Cup, saucer.
Seaham Pottery.

(**Forget and Forgive;** see 293).

71

Forget me not

    (motto only; see also 240).

Jug.
?'Garrison'

72

Forget not Christ the Lord of Hosts
Your pilot's captain, friend
For he will safely steer your course
And guide you to the end

'Garrison'

73

Forgive and Forget

Forgive and forget is a maxim sublime
But I've learnt but one half of it yet
The theft of my heart I can freely forgive
But the thief I can never forget

    (see also 76, 293).

74

For man dieth and wasteth away, yea man
giveth up the ghost and where is he
(Job: 14, 40)

Love-Feast Cup, plaque.
'Garrison'

74a

Freemason's Arms

    (transfer design).

Jug.

75

A Friend that is social goodnatured and free
To a pot of my liquor right welcome shall be
But he that is proud & illnatured may pass
By my door to an alehouse & pay for his glass.

Loving-cup.
?Scott.

76

Forgive and Forget

Friends are like leaves,
Which on the trees do grow
In summers prosperous state
Much love do show
But when in adversity then they
Like leaves in autumn fall away.

Jug.
Moore, 'Garrison'

(Friendship, Love and Truth; see 313).

77

A Frigate in Full Sail

    (title below transfer of ship).

Bowl.
Moore, 'Garrison'

78

From fire and damp
And every ill
May God preserve
The pitman still

Jug, dated 1824.

79

From hence in the deep
May divisions be tos'd
And prudence recover
What folly has lost

Jug, dated 1836.
'Garrison'.
Jug.
Dawson.

80

From rocks and sands
And barren lands
Kind fortune keep me free;
And from great guns,
And women's tongues;
Good Lord deliver me

Bowl.
Moore.

81

From rocks and sands
And every ill
May God preserve
The sailor still

82

Gamecock

    (design, with motto; see 302).

Jug.
Scott.

83

Gardener's Arms

    (title below transfer).

Jug.
'Garrison'

84

Garibaldi

    (title below transfer portrait).

Bowl.
Scott, 'Garrison'

85

The Gauntlet Clipper Ship

    (title below transfer of ship).

Bowl.
'Garrison'

86

Gentlemen now try your skill
I'll hold your sixpence if you will
That you don't drink unless you spill

Mug, two-handled.

(The Gift; see 149).

87

Give not thyself to indolence
Want of care is want of virtue

Ball.

88

Glide on my bark the summers tide,
Is gently flowing by thy side;
Around thy prow the waters bright
In circling rounds of broken light
Are glitt'ring as if ocean gave
Her countless gems to deck the wave

    (variations occur).

Mug.
'Garrison'.

Bowl.
Moore, Scott.

89

GOD
be merciful to me a
SINNER
Luke XVIII, 13

Plaque.

90

God is keeping me
and the gift giver
hopes for ever.

Plaque, dated 1849.

91

God is Love

Plaque.

(God is our Guide; see 178).

(God is with us; see 23, 308).

92

To R. Cobden
God said let there be light and lo
Light sprang forth at his word
God said let there be bread, but know;
Man did not heed the Lord.
But Cobden rose like wisdoms star
From Knowledge's bright sea,
And knaves were hushed and tyrants crushed
And labour's bread was free

Mug.
'Garrison'

93

God speed the plough

    (motto only. It sometimes appears below Farmer's Arms; see 64).

(God Save the Queen; see 194).

94

Going into Port

    (title below a ship transfer)

Plate
'Garrison'

95

Flowers that Never Fade

Good Humour

Good humour is the greatest charm
That children can possess
It makes them happy & what's more
It gives them power to bless

Mug.
Newbottle.

96

A Good name is rather
to be chosen than
great riches

    (Proverbs: XII, 1)

Butterdish.
Ball.

(The Goose with the Golden Egg; see 200a).

97

Gothic

    (design on tableware).
'Garrison'

(Grace after Meat; see 309).

98

The Great Australian Clipper Ship

    (title below transfer of ship).

Bowl.
Moore.

98a

The Great Bridge over the valley of the River
Wear; in the line of the Durham Junction Railway.
Length 810 feet 9 in. Mr. Harrison engineer.
Mr. Gibb builder, height 157 feet.

    (appears below transfer-printed view of the Victoria Railway
    Bridge at Penshaw).

Mug.
'Garrison'

99

The Great Eastern Steam-Ship

    (title below transfer of the steamship).

Bowl.
Scott, Moore.

100

Grog is the seaman's delight, his sheet anchor
His cable, his compass, his log,
It gives him a heart life's cares cannot canker
For he braves them and tips up his grog.

    (a rendering of Dibdin's 'Sailor's Sheet Anchor').

Jug.
'Garrison'

101

The Gypsies' Pastime

(title below transfer design).

Bowl.
Scott.

101a

Hail Masonry divine
Glory of Ages, shine
Long may thou reign
Where're thy Lodges stand
May they have great command
And always grace the land
Thou ART divine

Masonic Jug.
Dawson.

(This can be sung to the National Anthem).

102

The Smith's Arms
Hammer [sic] and Hand
All arts do stands [sic]

Jug.
'Garrison'

103

The Hardy Sailor
The hardy sailor braves the ocean
Fearless of the roaring wind
Yet his heart, with soft emotion,
Throbs to leave his love behind.
To dread of foreign foes a stranger,
Through the youth can dauntless roam,
Alarming fears paint every danger
In a rival left at home.

Bowl.
?'Garrison'

104

Have communion with few,
Be familiar with one,
Deal justly with all
Speak evil of none

(see also 21).

(variant: **to** for **with** in line 3).

Jug, mug.
'Garrison'

104a

Health and Independency

Jug.
?'Garrison'

105

Health to the sick,
Honour to the brave,
Success to the lover
And freedom to the slave.

Bowl.
Ball.

106

Hear not ill of a friend
Nor speak any of an enemy

Ball.

106a

A heart that conceals
And a tongue that never reveals

Masonic Mug.
?'Garrison'.

107

Hearts of oak are our ships
Hearts of oak are our men
We always are ready
Steady . . . boys, steady,
We'll fight and we'll conquer again and again

108

Merrily round the Capstan
Heave Oh Cherrily men, Heave Oh Heave

(see also 279).

Frog-mug.
Ball.

109

The Sailor's Tear
He leaped into the boat
As it lay upon the strand,
But, Oh! his heart was far away
With friends upon the land.
He thought of those he loved the best.
A wife and infant dear
And feeling filled the sailor's breast
The sailor's eye, a tear.

Jug.
'Garrison', Ball.

110

Here's a present for the lady
And a health to the bride
And the gentlemen that likes her
May good luck embrace them on every side

111

Success to the Coal Trade
Here's may colliers flourish, our trade increase
And victory bring us a lasting peace

Mug.
'Garrison'.

112

Here's success attend the farmer
And success to the fleece
May we be taxed less
And our commerce increase

'Garrison'.

113

Here's to the wind that blows
And the ship that goes
And the boy that fears no danger
A ship in full sail
And a fine pleasant gale
And the girl that loves a sailor.

(paraphrase of the chorus of the 'Lass that Loves a Sailor' by
Charles Dibden (1745-1814)).

Jug, mug.
'Garrison'.

114

Here's to you
And all your crew
Men and boys
And captain too.

Jug.
'Garrison'.

115

Here's to you, Jack,
With all my heart,
We'll have a glass
Before we part
Success to the tars of old England

116

He that believeth shall be saved

Love-Feast Cup.
'Garrison'.

117

He that by the plough would thrive,
Himself must either hold or drive.

(Benjamin Franklin: 'Poor Richard' [1747]).

Mug, two-handled.
'Garrison'.

118

He that refuseth instruction
Dispiseth his own soul

Bowl.
Ball.

118a

The Trumpeter taken Prisoner

He who incites the strife is worse than he who takes part in it.

Bowl.
Moore.

119

Holiness to the Lord.

Jug, sauce boat.
'Garrison'.

120

Holy bible, Book divine,
Precious treasure thou art mine.
Mine to tell me whence I came
Mine to teach me what I am.

Mug.
?'Garrison'.

120a

Home is a name of more than magic spell
Whose sacred power the wanderer best can tell
He who far distant from his native land
Feels at her name his eager soul expand
Whether as Patriot, Husband, Father, Friend
To that dear point his only wishes tend
And yet owns where'er his footsteps roam
Life's choicest blessings centre all at HOME.

Jug.
Dawson.

121

Honi soit qui mal y pense

Mug.

121a

Hope

(title below classical female standing figure, holding her attribute,
an anchor, ships beyond).

Bowl.
Scott.

(**The Horse and the Ass,** see 53a).

122

How grand in age,
How fair in youth,
Is holy Friendship,
Love and Truth

(this also sometimes appears as a couplet at the end of 313).

123

How happy every child of grace,
Who knows his sin forgiven!
This earth, he cries, is not my place,
I seek my place in heaven;
A country far from mortal sight;
Yet, O! by faith I see
The land of rest, the saints' delight
The heaven prepared for me.

Jug.
?'Garrison'.

124

Hunting Scene

(transfer design).

Plaque, bowl.
Moore.

125

The Sailor Boy
I am the lad in the blue and white,
Sing Hey! the merry sailor boy,
I carry my country's flag and name;
I never do her wrong or shame;
I'll fight her battles and share her fame
Sing Ho! the gallant sailor boy

Frog-mug.
Moore, Ball.

126

I do not know what man to trust
Since man to man is so unjust
I trusted many to my sorrow
So pay today
I'll trust tomorrow

Jug.
'Garrison'.

127

I envy no ones birth or fame,
Their title, train or dress,
Nor has my pride ever stretched its aim
Beyond what I possess.
I ask not, wish not to appear,
More beauteous, rich or gay.
Lord make me wiser every year
And better every day.

   (Charles Lamb: 'A Birthday Thought').

Mug, jug.
'Garrison'.

Jug.
Scott.

128

If it be possible
Live in peace with all men

Ball.

129

Flowers that never Fade

Politeness

If little boys and girls were wise
They'd always be polite,
For sweet behaviour in a child
Is a delightful sight

Plate.
Newbottle.

130

If solid happiness we prize,
Within our hearts this jewel lies;
And they are fools who roam,
The world has little to bestow,
From our dear selves our joys must flow,
Our bliss begins at home.

We'll relish therefore with content
What e'er kind providence has sent,
Nor aim beyond our power.
And if our store of wealth be small
With thankful hearts improve it all
Nor waste the present hour.

   (examples are found with only the first stanza).

Jug.
Ball.

131

If there be a will
There is mostly a way

Ball.

132

The Token, or Jack's Safe Return to his True Love
If you loves I as I loves you
No pair so happy as we two

   (from 'The Token' by Charles Dibden [1745-1814].

   (this title and couplet appear on a transfer showing a sailor embracing a young woman and clutching what has been described as a 'bath sponge'. It is in fact a hot-cross bun, which was baked by the sailor's wife or sweetheart and given to him at the beginning of a voyage. The bun was kept in the man's sea-chest throughout the voyage as a mascot against death by drowning).

Bowl.
Scott, Ball.

133

The Tythe Pig

In a country village lives a vicar
Fond as all are of Tythes and Liquer,
To mirth his ears are seldom shut
He'll crack a joke and laugh at smut.
But when his tythes he gathers in
True Parson then, no coin no grin
On fish on flesh on birds and beast
Alike lays hold the churlish priest
Hal's wife and sow as Gossips tell
Both at a time in pieces fell
The parson comes the Pig he claims
And the good wife with taunts inflames
But she quite arch bow'd low and smil'd
Kept back the pig and held out the child
The Priest look'd gruff the wife look'd big
Z. . . ds Sir quoth she No Child no Pig

Jug.
North Hylton, 'Garrison'.

134

Flowers that never Fade

Meekness

In a modest, humble mind,
God himself will take delight,
But the proud & haughty find,
They are hateful in his sight

Plate.
Newbottle.

135

In conversation with a friend,
A social hour to pass,
I'll not forget my latter end
How swift is time alass; [sic]
With caution walk our future way
Our work will soon be done,
Let Friendship reign while here we stay
And evil speak of none.

Jug.
'Garrison'.

136

Independent Order of Oddfellows — Manchester Unity

(between the two mottoes, a pair of clasped hands. Design of arms, engraved by Moses Ryles, on reverse).

Mug, dated 1841, Plate.
Dawson.

137

In God is our Trust

Jug.
Scott.

138

**In Thee O Lord do I put my trust
Let me never be confounded.**

Plaque.
'Garrison'.

139

Look Aloft

In the tempest of life
When the wave and the gale
Are around and above
If thy footing should fail
If thine eye should grow dim
And thy caution depart
"Look aloft" and be firm
And be fearless of heart

Jug.
Ball.

139a

**In this jug there is good liquor
Fit for either priest or vicar
But to drink and not to spill
Will try the utmost of your skill.**

Puzzle Jug.
'Garrison'.

140

The I.O.U. of Mechanics

(title above transfer of coat of arms).

Mug.
'Garrison'.

(Jack Crawford, the Hero of Camperdown; see 50).

(Jack Crawford, the true British Sailor; see 16).

(Jack on a Cruise; see 18).

141

Jack on a Cruise

(title below transfer of sailor and sweetheart).

Mug.
'Garrison'.

142

Jack's Safe Return

(title below transfer design of sailor and sweetheart, without couplet; see also 132).

Mug.
Scott.

(John Crawford; see 51).

142a

January

(title above transfer design on 'months' bowl; see also 199).

Scott.

143

John Gilpin's Ride

(transfer design).

Dawson.

144

**John Wright Wayman
Mayor of Sunderland 1883 & 1884**

(title below transfer portrait).

Jug.
Ball.

144a

July

(title above transfer design on 'months' bowl; see also 199).

Scott.

144b

June

(title above transfer design on 'months' bowl; see also 199).

Scott.

145

**Keep company with such as may
make thee wiser and better**

Ball.

146

Keep Holy the Sabbath Day

(inscription in relief on rim of plate; see 10, 134).

Newbottle.

147

**Keep me clean and use me well
And what I see I will not tell**

(see 282).

Chamber Pot.
'Garrison'.

148

Key Border

(design on dinner ware).

Moore.

149

The Gift

Kindly take this gift of mine
The gift and giver I hope is thine
And tho' the value is but small
A loving heart is with it all

Bowl.
Moore.

150

Ladies all
I pray make free
And tell me how
You like my tea

(variant **your** in last line on 'Garrison' jug).

Jug.
Scott, Newbottle.

151

Lake with two swans

(design on tableware)

'Garrison'.

(**The Landlord's Caution;** see 31).

152

Landscape with classical ruin and pyramid of Caius Cestius, Rome

(design on tableware).

Plate.
Dawson.

153

Landscape with fishermen

(design on tableware).

'Garrison'.

154

Landscape with temple and palm trees

(design on plaques).

'Garrison'.

155

Lay things by
They may come into use

Ball.

156

Let Brotherly love continue

Jug, mug.
'Garrison'.

157

Let Love abide
Till death divide

Jug, dated 1839.

158

Let masonry from pole to pole
After sacred laws expand
Far as the mighty waters roll
To wash remotest land
That virtue has not left mankind
Her social maxims prove
For stamped upon the mason's mind
Are unity and love

Jug.
'Garrison'.

159

Let others worship Glittering Dust
And boast of earthly toys;
Christ is my rock my hope my trust
And spring of all my joys

Mug, dated 1837.
'Garrison'.

160

Let no obligation to thy
Friend engage thee to dispense
with thy conscience

Ball.

161

Let reason be your pilot
When pashon [sic] blows the gale
And virtue be your helmsman
When Love doth fill the sail

Jug.

162

Let the wealthy and great
Roll in splendor and state,
I envy them not I declare it
I eat my own lamb
My chicken and ham
I shear my own fleece and I wear it.
I have fruits I have flowers
I have lawns I have bowers
The lark is my morning alarmer.
So joly [sic] boys now
Here's God speed the plough
Long life and success to the farmer

(see also 64).

Jug.
Scott, Ball.

163

Let thy failings and thy faults be secrets; endeavour to mend them
but not to publish them

Ball.

164

Life Boat

   (title above transfer showing lifeboat rescue from a wrecked
   vessel; see 184a, 330b).

Jug, dated 1831.
'Garrison'.

165

Life's like a ship in constant motion
Sometimes high and sometimes low,
Where everyone must brave the ocean
Whatsoever winds may blow.
But if assailed by squall or shower
Or wafted by the gentle gales,
Let's not lose the favouring hour
But drink success unto the sails.

Bowl.
Scott, 'Garrison'.

166

Like pillars we stand
An immobile band,
Cemented by power from above.
Then freely let pass
The generous glass
To masonry, friendship and love.

167

Listen to all the world
rather than be ignorant of
any of thy faults

Ball.

168

A little Health, a little Wealth
A little house with freedom
And at the end, a little Friend
With little cause to need him

Jug.
'Garrison'.

(**Look Aloft**; see 139).

169

Long may we live
Happy may we be,
Blest with content,
From misfortune free.

Mug.
Phillips, Hylton.

170

The Lord is my shepherd my guardian and guide
Whatsoever I want he will kindly provide
Ever since I was born it is He that hath crowned
The life that He gave me with blessings around.

Mug.

   (a variant, on a Ball Bros. mug, is set out in 8 lines, substituting
   doth for **will**. This verse has been found on an early 19th century
   broadsheet in a scrapbook in Sunderland Museum, entitled 'Psalm
   23rd. Versified').

(**Lord Nelson Engaging the Toulon Fleet of** [sic] **the Mouths of the
Nile**; see 331).

171

The Lord unite us both in one,
And in His love may we agree,
To praise Him while on earth we live,
That after death may happy be.

Marriage Cup.
'Garrison'.

172

Lose not thine own for want
of asking for it: 'twill get
thee no thanks

Ball.

173

The loss of gold is great
The loss of health is more
But losing Christ is such a loss
As no man can restore.

Mug.
'Garrison'.

Jug.
Scott, Moore.

174

The loss of gold is much
The loss of health is more
The loss of Christ is such a loss
As no man can restore.

   (variant: **time** for **health**).

Jug.
'Garrison'.

(**Love**; see 280).

175

Love and Be Happy

Bowl.
?'Garrison'.

176

Love and Live, Happy

Mug.
?North Hylton.

177

Love not sleep
Lest thou come to poverty

Sugar basin.
Ball.

178

Loyal Independent Order of Oddfellows Arms

   (title below transfer with motto **God is our Guide**).

Plate.

120

179

Majestically slow before the breeze
The tall ship marches on the azure seas
In silent pomp she cleaves the watery plain
The pride and wonder of the billowy main

Jug.
'Garrison'.

(this verse appears below a transfer-printed design of three sailing ships which bears the signature 'Downing Sc.'. This may be the work of William Downing, an engraver known to be working in Staffordshire. c. 1800-1811).

180

Make not a jest of truth

Ball.

181

Manchester Unity Independent Order of Odd Fellow [sic]

Bowl.
?Moore.

182

Manchester Unity. Independent Order of Odd Fellows

(titles below transfers of Coats of Arms; see also 136).

Bowl.
Scott, Ball.

183

Manchester Unity of Oddfellows

(title below transfer).

Butter dish.
Ball.

184

The Sailor's Tear

The man doomed to sail
With the blast of the gale;
Through billows atlantic to steer
As he bend o'er the wave
Which may soon be his grave
He remembers his home with a tear.

Bowl.
'Garrison'.

Mug.
Scott.

184a

The Life Boat

Man the lifeboat! Man the lifeboat!
Hearts of oak your succour lend,
See the shattered vessel staggers
Quick, oh quick assistance send
See the ark of refuge launching
See Her hardy crew prepare
For the dangerous work of heroes
Gallant British hearts are there.

184b

March

(title above transfer design on 'months' bowl; see also 199).

Scott.

185

Mariner's Arms
Deus Dabit Vela

(title and motto below transfer).

Bowl.
Moore.

Mug.
'Garrison'.

186

Mariner's Compass

(title below transfer).

Bowl.
Moore.

Mug,
'Garrison'.

(one version of this transfer design is signed ''Eng. for J. Phillips & Co. Sunderland Pottery, Robson sculpt''. Thomas Robson of Sunderland [died c.1869] was an engraver of considerable skill, producer of several local maps, prints, bookplates, etc., and the author of *The British Herald*. This book, published in Sunderland in 1850, is a fine example of typography and engraving).

(Marriage; see 282).

187

Masonic Arms

(title below transfer).

Jug, bowl, mug.
Scott, 'Garrison'.

188

Mason's Arms

(title below transfer).

Mug.
'Garrison'.

189

Mate Sound the Pump
Morning, Noon and Night

Plaque.
'Garrison', Ball.

190

Mather, Minister of the Pledge

(title below transfer portrait).

Saucer, cup.
?'Garrison'.

190a

May Carpenters flourish and our trade increase
And victory bring lasting peace.

Jug.
Dawson.

190b

May

(title above transfer design on 'months' bowl; see also 199).

Scott.

191

May friendship reign
And discord cease;
And all Oddfellows
Live in peace

192

May Orangemen true
Their rights pursue
Whilst honour crowns their cause;
Their church and King
And every Thing
That constitutes their laws

Mug.
Scott.

Jug.
'Garrison'.

193

May peace and Plenty
On our nation smile,
& trade and commerce
Bless the British Isle

Bowl.
'Garrison'.

Jug.
Dawson.

(variant **with commerce**, line 3 on 'Garrison' mug).

194

Crimea

May they ever be united
Vive L'empereur
God save the Queen

Jug, bowl, mug.
Scott.

Bowl.
Moore.

(also appears below a transfer of British and French flags, supported by sailors).

Jug.
Ball.

195

May they ever be United

(motto above a design with portraits of Napoleon III [left] and Queen Victoria [right] amid flags and heraldic creatures and surmounted by an eagle).

Jug.
?Moore.

196

Medina

(design on tableware).

'Garrison'.

(Meekness; see 134).

(Merrily round the Capstan; see 108, 279).

197

Mild charity's glow
To us mortals below
Shows the soul from barbarity clear,
Compassion will melt
Where the virtue's felt,
And its dew is diffused with a tear.

Hollow pot ball.
Moore.

198

The Milk-Fetching Dog

(title below transfer design showing a dog sitting before a door on which is written 'Milk and Cream sold Here').

Bowl.
Scott.

(The Miser; see 330a).

199

The Months

(The inscriptions January, February, etc. appear on jugs and bowls).

Scott.

200

Mosaic

(design on fancy wares).

Scott.

200a

The Goose with the Golden Egg
Much warrants more and loses all.

Bowl.
Moore.

200b

My bonny sailor is on my mind
My heart is now with him at sea
I hope the summer's western breeze
Will bring him safely back to me.

201

My heart is fixed
I cannot range
I like my choice
Too well to change

Double frog-mug, jug.
'Garrison'.

202

My lad is far upon the sea
His absence makes me mourn
The bark that bears him far from me
I hope will safe return

And from his earnings I'll save up
If lucky he should be
And then when old with me shall stop
And go no more to sea.

Jug.
?'Garrison'.

203

My ship is moored
My wages paid
So let me haste
Unto my maid

(see 249).

Jug.
'Garrison'.

204

Napoleon

(transfer design).

Plaque, jug.
Dawson.

205

Nelson's Fleet off the Nile

(title below transfer).

Mug.
Dawson.

206

Nelson's Victory

(transfer design of ship).

Plaque.
Moore.

206a

The new railway bridge Sunderland.

(title below transfer-printed view of Monkwearmouth Railway
Bridge, opened 1879).

Jug.
Ball.

207

Nonpareil

(design on tableware).

'Garrison'.

(Norah Creina Steam Yacht; see 52).

208

The Northumberland '74

(title below transfer of ship).

Jug, plaque.
'Garrison'.

208a

November

(title above transfer design on 'months' bowl; see also 199).

Scott.

209

The Sailor's Return

Now safe returned from dangers past
With joy I hail the shore
And fear no more the tempest's blast
Nor ocean's angry roar

Bowl.
Scott, 'Garrison', Moore, Ball.

209a

No words or waves our progress check
Our course we must pursue
And though the vessel fears a wreck
She's sav'd with all her crew

And when the trying time is o'er
And then my comforts do'st restore?
I'll to the praise of God declare
What Grace humbles Man to bear.

210

Now weigh the anchor hoist the sail,
Launch out upon the pathless deep,
Resolved however veer the gale
The destined port in mind to keep.
Through all the dangers of the way
Deliver us Good Lord we pray

(variant **veers**, line 3).

Bowl.
Moore, Scott, 'Garrison', Ball.

210a

October

(title above transfer design on 'months' bowl; see also 199).

Scott.

211

Oddfellows' Arms

(title below transfer; see also 178, 181-3).

Jug, plate.
Scott.

212

The Farmer

O happy is the farmer and free from all care
Who rises each morning to breath [sic] fresh air
And hears the bird's singing from every green bough.
No lifs [sic] like the farmers that follows the plough,
Success ere attend him and plenty and peace
May the seeds that he sows with blessings encrese [sic]
May health still around him its comforts bestow
Long life to the farmer and God speed the plough

Bowl, plaque.
'Garrison'.

212a

Oh! Dear Me! What do I see!

Chamber Pot.
'Garrison'.

(see 147, 282).

213

On boards and broken pieces toss'd
And death each hour at hand;
Yet through our pilot none are lost,
But all come safe to land

(On Time; see 289).

214

The order given the signal gun is fired
And the last moment of my stay expir'd.
In haste the deck I mount compared with me
The storm knows rest and peace the raging sea

(variants occur, *e.g.,* order's giv'n . . . fir'd).

Mug.
'Garrison'.
Jug.
Scott.

215

O that I could my Lord receive
Who did the world redeem
Who gave His life that I might live,
A life concealed in Him.
O that I could the blessing prove
My hearts extreme desire,
Live happy in my Saviour's love
And in His arms expire.

Mug.
Scott.

(Our trust is in God; see 255).
(below transfer of **Slaters' Arms**).

215a

Paul Jones

(title; transfer design of sailor standing beside cannon)

Jug.
'Garrison'.

216

The Pensioner's Yarn

(title below transfer design).

Plate.
Scott.

217

Points of the Compass

(transfer design).

Dawson, 'Garrison'.

(**Politeness**; see 129).

218

The poor opprest honest man
Had surely ne'er been born
Had there not been some recompence
To comfort those that mourn

219

Praise Ye the Lord

Plaque and plate.
'Garrison'.

220

Prepare to meet Thy God/Lord

Plaque.
'Garrison'.

221

A present for my dear Girl

222

A Present from Sunderland

Plate.
'Garrison'.

223

Primitive House

(painted design on cups and saucers).

Dawson.

224

The Ascent of the Aerial Balloon
Producing the bark to tan the hide off Buonaparte

Mug, jug.
Phillips, Hylton.

224a

Queen Victoria

(transfer-printed portrait c. 1838).

Mug.
'Garrison'.

224b

Ready the spirit of His Love
Just now the stony to remove
To apply and witness with the blood
And wash, and seal the Sons of God.

Mug.
'Garrison'.

225

Reindeer

(design on plates).

Moore.

226

Rejoice in the Lord

Plaque.
'Garrison'.

227

Rely not on another when thou
Can'st as well do it thyself

Ball.

228

Remember me,
When this you see,
And keep me in your mind,
For let the world
Say what they will,
Speak on me as you will find.

(variant: **of** occurs in last line).

Bowl.
'Garrison', Scott.

(Remembrance; see 270).

229

Respect men more for their goodness
than for their greatness

Ball.

(Rest in Heaven; see 277).

230

Retribution Steamer

(title below ship transfer).

Plaque.

231

Riflemen

(title below transfer of soldier saluting, amid cannon and barrels
marked 'powder').

Bowl.
Scott.

232

Romantic Landscape

(transfer design).
Tableware, wall tile.

Dawson.

233

The rose in June is not so sweet
As lovers kisses when they meet

234

Rose of Sharon

(design on tableware).

Moore.

235

Royal Cottage

(design on dinner ware).
'Garrison'.

236

Royal Nursery Polka

(transfer design).

Plate.
Dawson.

237

Sailing Ships

(transfer design of group of vessels, signed 'Downing Sc.' Often
occurs above verse 179).

Mug, jug.
'Garrison'.

(The Sailor Boy; see 125).

(The Sailor's Farewell; see 63, 240 and 271).
(this also occurs as a title below a transfer, without verse).

238

A sailor's life's the life for me,
He takes his duty merrily,
If winds can whistle, he can sing
Still faithful to his friend and king.
He gets beloved by all the ship.
And toasts his girl and drinks his flip

Mug.

239

Sailors now are tossed about
On life's tempestuous main
But grace assures beyond a doubt
They shall their port attain

?'Garrison'.

(The Sailor's Return; see 209).

(The Sailor's Tear; see 109, 184).

240

The Sailor's Farewell

(variant **Forget me Not,** used by Moore).

The sailor tost in stormy seas
Though far his bark may roam,
Still hears a voice in every breeze,
That wakens thoughts of home.
He thinks upon his distant frrends [sic]
His wife his humble cot
And from his inmost heart ascends,
The prayer forget me not

Jug.
'Garrison'.
Bowls.
Scott, Moore, Ball.

241

The sails unfurl let the billows curl
The north wind bleak we brave
And strangers to fear our wild course we steer
Thro' the foam of the wintry wave.
Let the hurricane howl be it fair or foul,
Our ardour nought can check,
On the giddy top-mast we sing to the blast
Or dance on the sea-washed deck

(first line variant: **Let the sails unfurl**).

Bowl.
Moore.

242

St. George's Mission, Hartley Street

(title below transfer design of Hartley Street Chapel, Sunderland).

Mug.
?Ball.

242a

St. Nicholas Church, Newcastle.

(title below transfer-printed view).

Jug.
Ball.

243

The Saviour of mankind adopts
The figure of the Hen
To show the strength of His regard
For the lost souls of men

'Garrison'.

244

Say if no more in converse sweet,
The blissful hours shall flee;
Or if that we no more may meet,
Wilt thou remember me.
No time shall change my firm regard,
Or banish thoughts of thee;
Oh! I will feel a sweet regard
If thou'll remember me.

Jug.
North Hylton.

244a

Says Sylvia to a reverend priest
What reason can be given
Since marriage is a holy thing
That there is none in heaven?
There are no women he replied
She quite returned the jest
Women there are, but I'm afraid
They can not find a priest.

(variant **friar** occurs in the first line).

Jug.
'?Garrison'.

245

Sea Flower

(the first Danish steamship).

Moore.

246

The Seasons

(The inscriptions Spring, Summer, etc., are found on figures of the Seasons).

'Garrison'.

246a

Seek ye the Lord

Plaque, bowl.
'Garrison', Ball.

246b

September

(title above transfer design on 'months' bowl; see also 199).

Scott.

247

Ship

(title below transfer of ship).

Ball.

248

Ship in Full sail

(title below transfer design).

'Garrison'.

249

The ship is moored
The wages paid
Welcome the sailor
To his maid

(see 203).

Jug.
'Garrison'.

250

Show me the wife that's on the watch
For every little rent or scratch
And cures it with a timely patch
Before you know it.
She is a woman fit to match
A lord or poet

251

Shun engagements, this is one of the chief maxims of prudence

Ball.

252

Since life's a jest we'll jest at life
And make a jest of sorrow
For why should we 'gainst life's decree
Be thoughtful of tomorrow.
At jest we laugh then laugh at life
For life is but a jest
And he who loves and laughs the most
Is he who lives the best.

Jug.
'Garrison'.

253

Sinners obey the gospel word
Haste to the supper of thy Lord
Be wise to know your gracious day
All things are ready, come away

Plaque.
'Garrison'.

254

Sir Francis Burdett

Independent Champion of British Freedom

> (b.1770, d.1844. In 1810 he was imprisoned in the Tower in consequence of a letter published in Cobbett's 'Political Register'. M.P. for Westminster, 1807-37).

Mug.
'Garrison'.

254a

Sit Lux et Lux Fuit

Masonic Jug.
?Dawson.

255

Slaters' Arms

> (with motto: **Our Trust is in God**).

Jug.
'Garrison'.

(**The Smith's Arms**; see 102).

256

Sons of Britain hear my story
Mercy well becomes the brave
Humanity is Britains glory
Oh pity and protect the slave

Free born daughters who possessing
Eyes that conquer hearts that save
Greet me with a sisters blessing
Oh pity and protect the slave

> (hand written).

Jug.
'Garrison'.

257

Sporting

> (transfer design).

Plaque.
Moore.

258

Star

> (transfer design).

Dawson.

259

Star of Tasmania

> (transfer of ship built 1856, Aberdeen. She was of 632 tons).

Moore.

260

Still as through life our weary steps we bend
Let us not think when beating storms descend
Still let religion hold unrivall'd sway
And patience walk companion of our way
And lose not sight of that delightful shore
Where blissful bowers shall friends to friends restore.

Jug.

260a

Success to all lovers
And may they prove true
May their pleasures be many
Their sorrows be few
Long may they live
And be happy together
And never be parted
Till death do them sever.

Jug.
?'Garrison'.

261

Success to all sailors
Their sweethearts and wives
May they never want money
All the days of their lives

Jug, dated 1839.

262

Success to all sailors

> (title above design of seated female figure, left, with ships, etc., right).

Mug.
Dawson.

Success to the Coal Trade; see 111).

263

Success to the farmer and prosper his plough
Rewarding his ardent toil all the year through
Seed time and harvest he ever shall get
He's trusted all to providence and so may he yet

> (variant: **He's trust**).

Bowl.
Scott, 'Garrison', Moore.

264

Success to the Fishermen

> (transfer motto).

Bowl.
Moore, Scott.

265

Success to the Fleece,
To the Plough and the Sail,
May our Taxes grow Less
And our Commerce ne'er fail

Plate.
?'Garrison'.

266

Success to the plow (plough) (both occur)
And jolly to the pale
May the landlord never flourish
Nor the tennent [sic] never fail

Jug.
'Garrison'.

267

Sunderland Coal Trade

(caption, surmounted by a crown, on a ribbon).

Jug.
Dawson.

(Sunderland Life Boat; see 330b).

268

Sunderland Volunteer Life Brigade

(title below transfer).

Mug, plate.
Scott.

269

The sun is up we'll brush the dew
And hear the huntsmans gay hulloo (variant: **halloo**)
And hark the dogs enlivening cry
Now see the horsemen gallop by
And now we hear the distant horn
Upon the dying echoes borne
From copse to copse the hunters hie
On hearing Drivers well known cry

Jug, mug.
Scott.

Bowl.
Ball, 'Garrison'.

270

Remembrance

The sun shall lose its splendour,
The tides shall cease to flow,
And tyrant's heart grow tender,
And melt at others' woe.
The frosty breath December
Shall blight the flower of May
Ere I cease to remember
The friends now far away

Bowl.

(Susan's Farewell; see 2).

271

The Sailor's Farewell

Sweet Oh! Sweet is that sensation,
Where two hearts in union meet,
But the Pain of Separation,
Mingles bitter with the Sweet

(variant of **when** for **where** in second line also occurs).

Bowl, mug.
Moore.

Mug.
Scott.

272

Swiftly see each moment flies,
See and learn be timely wise,
Every moment shortens day,
Every pulse beats life away,
Thus thy every heaving breath,
Wafts thee on to certain death,
Seize the moments as they fly,
Know to live and learn to die

Bowl, chamber pot.
'Garrison'.
Bowl.
Scott.

273

Teach me to feel another's woe
To hide the fault I see
That mercy I to others show
That mercy show to me

('The Universal Prayer', Alexander Pope (1688-1740)).

Butter dish.
'Garrison'.

274

Tea-Party

(design on tea-sets).

'Garrison'.

275

Tell me ye knowing and discerning few,
Where I may find a friend both just and true,
Who dare stand by me when in deep distress,
And then his love and friendship do most express

Jug.
Dawson.

275a

Temperance

(inscription in relief on rim of plate with verse 129).

Plate.
Newbottle.

276

Then on this stream of time thy vessel glide
And pure as heaven the waters seem to roll
Ere long in calm or tempest shall the tide
Cast on a land unknown thy naked soul.
Ah then when life and death no more shall be
Where reader wilt thou spend eternity.

277

Rest in Heaven

There is an hour of peaceful rest
To mourning wand'rers given;
There is a tear for souls distrest
A balm for every wounded breast
Tis found above in Heaven

Jug.
'Garrison', Phillips, Hylton.

278

There's a frigate on the waters,
Fit for battle, storm, or fun,
She dances like a lifeboat,
Though she carries flag and gun,
What'er [sic] may try, she'll stand the test,
The brave, the staunch, the free,
She bears a name of stainless fame,
The Fairy of the sea.

Bowl.
?Ball.

Jug.
'Garrison'.

279

Merrily round the Capstan

There's one whose fearless courage
Yet has never failed in fight,
Who gaurds [sic] with zeal our country's weal.
Our freedom and our right.
He's Britains Bost [sic] and claims a tost [sic]
In peace my boys or war.
Heres to the brave upon the wave,
The gallant English tar.

Frog-mug, bowl.
Ball.

280

Love

There's sunshine on the sea my love,
There's beauty o'er the skies,
But fairer seem thy looks my love
And brighter are thine eyes

(this verse also appears without title).

Bowl.
Ball.

Jug.
?Moore.

280a

The Ass in the Lion's Skin

They who assume a character that does not belong to them generally betray themselves by over acting it.

Bowl.
Moore.

281

This is a good world to live in
To lend or to spend or to give in
But to beg or to borrow
Or get a man's own
It is such a world
As never was known

(a first line variant **This world is a good one to live in,** with the last four lines set out as two; see also 290).

Bowls.
North Hylton, ?Ball.

282

Marriage

This pot it is a present sent
Some mirth to make is only meant
We hope the same you'll not refuse
But keep it safe and oft it use
When in it you want to p-ss [sic]
Remember them that gave you THIS

(see also 147).

Chamber pot.
'Garrison'.

(variant last line: **them who sent** [Ball]).

(This world is a good one to live in; see 281).

283

Though malt and venom
Seem united
Don't break my pot
Or be affrighted

Frog-mug, plaque.
Moore.

(A mug in a private collection has the added stanza:

For when its full
No spleen is seen
And when its empty
It's quite clean)

284

Thou, God, See'st Me

Plaque, mug.
'Garrison'.

285

Thou hold'st thy course in independent pride,
No leave asked thou of either wind or tide,
'Tis whate'er point the breeze constant veer,
Still doth thy careful helmsman onward steer.
As if the stroke of some magicians wand,
Had lent power the ocean to command

Bowl.

286

Thou noble bark of brightest fame,
That bear'st proud England's honoured name,
Right welcome home once more,
Welcome, thou gallant little sail
In Englands name I bid the [sic] hail
And welcome to her shore

'Garrison', Scott, Moore.

287

Thus sailing at peril on sea or on shore
We box the compass right cheerly
Toss the grog, boys, about and a song or two more
Then we'll drink to the girls we love dearly

Jug.
Moore, 'Garrison'.

('Garrison' has **old** before **compass** in line 2).

288

Thus smiling at sea or on shore
We box the old compass right cheerly
Toss the can, boys, about and a word or two more
Yes, drink to the girls we love dearly;
For sailors, pray mind the strange kind of fish
Love the girls just as dear as there [sic] mother;
And what's more, they love what I hope you all wish
'Tis the heart that can feel for another

Frog-mug.

289

On Time

Time was in past thou cans't not it recall
Time is thou has employ the portion small
Time future is not and may never be
Time present is the only time for thee

Bowl.
?Ball.

290

'Tis a very good world for to live in
To lend or to spend or to give in
But to beg or to borrow or get a man's own,
'Tis a very worst world that ever was known

    (see also 281).

Bowl.
?Scott, or Moore.

291

'Tis religion that can give
Sweetest pleasure while we live
'Tis religion must supply
Solid comfort when we die

    (from 'True Pleasures' by Mary Masters, in 'Gems of Song for the Sunday School', 1869).

Jug.
'Garrison'.

292

'Tis Religion that gives Sweetest Pleasure

Plaque.
'Garrison'.

(**Tithe Pig**; see 133).

293

Forget and Forgive

To forgive and forget is a maxim of old
Tho I've learnt but one half of it yet
The theft of my heart I can freely forgive
But the thief I can never forget

    (see also 73 & 76).

Mug.
Ball.

(**The Token**; see 132).

294

Too oft is the smile
But the hypocrites wile
To mark detestation or fear
Give me the soft sigh
Whilst the soul telling eye
Is dimmed for a time with a tear

Jug.
Scott, Moore.

    (variant: **a** for **the** in line 2).

(**To R. Cobden**; see 92).

(**Trafalgar**; see 33).

294a

Tournament

    (transfer design).

Plaque.
Moore.

295

A Trifle for Frances

    (hand written).

Jug.

296

A Trifle for my child

    (impressed in relief on the rim of plate, with verse 129).

Newbottle.

297

The troubled main, the wind and rain,
By ardent passions prove,
Lash'd to the helm, should seas o'erwhelm,
I'll think on thee, my love.

'Garrison'.

298

True Love from Hull

    (title below transfer of a barque).

Bowl.
Moore.

(**Tythe Pig**; see 133).

    (title below transfer design without verse).

Jug.
'Garrison'.

(**The Trumpeter taken Prisoner**; see 118a).

298a

Turkish Pavilion

    (transfer design).

Teapot.
'Garrison'.

298b

Tynemouth Haven

(transfer design).

Bowl.
?Ball.

299

The Unfortunate London

(title below transfer of ship).

Bowl.
Moore, Scott.

(The London, built in July, 1864, was wrecked in the Bay of Biscay, with the loss of over 300 lives, in 1865. Such pieces may thus be dated).

300

Unitas Benovelentiaet Concordia

(motto on scroll beneath a shield of arms, a huntsman at either side, one with dog).

Bowl.
Scott.

301

Victoria and Albert Yacht

(title below ship transfer).

Bowl.
Scott.

301a

A view of the cast iron bridge to be erected over the River Thames. Span of this arch 220 ft.; span of middle arch 240 ft.; height 100 ft.; span of this arch 220 ft.

(Signed 'E. Barker' (below left) and 'Sunderland' (below right)).

Jug.

301b

A view of the cast iron bridge to be erected over the River Thames. Span of middle arch 240 ft.; height 100 ft.; of the other two 220 ft.

Jug.

(Transfer-printed views of 301a and 301b show the iron bridge designed by John Rennie and erected over the River Thames at Southwark, 1816-1819).

302

Vigilans et Audax

(motto below transfer design of gamecock).

Jug.
Scott.

303

Virtue is the chiefest beauty
of the mind
The noblest ornament
of human kind
Virtue our safeguard
And our guideing [sic] star
That stirs up reason
when our senses err

Jug.
?Scott.

Mug.
Dawson.

(Vive L'Empereur; see 194).

304

Waverley

(transfer design).

Dinner ware, plaque.
Moore.

305

The weather's fair, the season's now
Drive on, my Boy, God speed the plough.

Jug.
Moore.

306

We sailors are born for all weathers
Great guns let them blow high blow low
Our duty keeps us to our tethers
And where the gale drives we must go

Jug.
Dawson.

307

John Wesley

(title below transfer portrait).

Plaque.
'Garrison'.

308

The Rev. John Wesley, A.M. Wesleyan Methodist Society established 1739

(title below transfer portrait of Wesley, above which is caption 23).

Mug.
Scott.

309

Grace after Meal

We thank Thee Lord for this our food
But more because of Jesus blood
Let manna to our souls be given
The bread of life sent down from Heaven

309a

The Dog in a Manger
What miserable cur who neither can eat corn himself or will
allow those to eat it who can.

Bowl.
Moore.

310

What should sailors do on shore
But kiss the girls and toss the can
When the cannons cease to roar
Sweet's the voice of smiling Nan

Jug.
Dawson.

    (the words 'Dawson and Co.' form part of the transfer).

311

What thou designest to do well
speedily put into practice.

Ball.

311a

Whene'er I see thy lovely face
My heart with joy doth burn
Whenever absent from the place
I long for thy return.

Jug.

312

When first I was a foremast man I often did pretend,
If ere I got promoted I'd be a seaman's friend,
But in a little time I was promoted to be mate,
I then like many others forgot my former state.
When I became a captain I thought myself a king,
I then entirely did forget the foremast man I'd been.

Bowl, jug.
Moore.

Jug.
?Scott, 'Garrison'.

313

Friendship, Love and Truth

When friendship love and truth abound
Among a band of brothers,
The air of joy goes sweetly round,
Each shares the bliss of others.
Sweet roses grace the thorny way,
Along this vale of sorrow,
The flowers that shed their leaves to-day,
Shall bloom again tomorrow.

Jug.

    (some examples have a final couplet added; see 122).

Ewer, jug.
'Garrison'.

314

When in solemn secret prayer
When your spirit finds access
When you breath [sic] in all your care
Sweetly at the throne of grace
Me to Jesus then commend
Think upon your absent friend

315

When riding o'er the mountain wave,
The Hardy, Sailor, ever brave,
He laughs at danger, smiles at fate,
And risks his life, to save his mate

Jug.
Ball.

316

When round the bowl the jovial crew
The early scenes of youth renew,
Tho each his favrite [sic] fair will boast,
This is the universal toast.
May we, when toil and danger's o'er,
Cast anchor on our native shore.

Jug.
'Garrison'.

317

When tempests mingle sea and sky
And winds like lions rage and rend
Ships o'er the mountain waters fly
Or down unfathom'd depths descend
Though skill avail not, strength decay
Deliver us good Lord we pray

Bowl.
Scott, Moore, Ball.

318

When this you see remember me,
And keep me in your mind,
Let all the world say what they will,
Speak of/on me as you find.

    (a variant has: When far at sea remember me and bear for keep
in line 2).

Mug.
Ball, Phillips, Hylton.

319

When this you see,
Remember me;
Though many miles,
We distant be.

Mug, dated 1837.
'Garrison'.

319a

Where mutual love betwixt man and Wife
Adorn the marriage station
It sweetens all the cares of life
And leaves no room for Passion.

320

Whoso mocketh the Poor
reproacheth his Maker

Plaque.
'Garrison'.

321

Wild Rose

    (design on dinner ware).

Dawson, Moore.

322

William IV

(title below transfer of sailing ship).

Jug.
'Garrison'.

323

Willie Wouldhave 1789

Inventor of the Lifeboat

(portrait of Wouldhave, surrounded by lifebelt, on which the above is written; see also 68).

Bowl.
Ball.

324

Willow Pattern

(design on tableware).

Dawson, Scott, Moore, 'Garrison', Seaham.

324a

Windsor Castle

(design on tableware).

Dish.
?Moore.

325

A wise son maketh a glad father

Butterdish.
Ball.

326

Wish not so much to live long as to live well

Ball.

327

Women make men love;
Love makes them sad;
Sadness makes them drink,
And drinking makes them mad.

Bowl.
Scott.

(. . . sets them mad)

(. . . drives them mad)

Mug.
'Garrison'.

328

The World Illusive

The world is all a fleeting Show,
For Man's illusion given;
The smiles of joy, the tears of woe,
Deceitful shine, deceitful flow,
There's nothing true but heaven.

Jug.
'Garrison'.

329

The world is in pain
Our secrets (secret) to gain
But still let them wonder and gaze on
They ne'er (never) can divine
The word nor (or) the sign
Of a free and an accepted mason

(incorporated in a design of masonic symbols; a variant occurs as shown).

Chamber pot.
'Garrison'.

Jug.
Phillips, Hylton.

330

The world's a city with many a crooked street;
And death's a market place where all men meet;
If life was merchandise which men could buy,
The rich would live, the poor alone would die

Jug.
'Garrison'.

(the first two lines a variation of two lines from Fletcher's play 'Two Noble Kinsmen', c. 1613. The four lines, with minor variations appear on a tombstone in Nutfield Church, Surrey, dated 1860). (This also occurs as on 8-line stanza).

330a

The Miser

The worth of money is not in its possession but in its use.

Bowl.
Moore.

330b

Sunderland Life Boat

Ye sea built castles wonders of the deep
Strike your proud tops
And here blush to see
One vessel sacred to humanity

Mug.
?'Garrison'

331

Lord Nelson Engaging the Toulon Fleet of [sic] the Mouths of
the Nile

The Young Alexander of France
May boast of his prowess in vain
When Nelson appears 'tis confes't
That Britons are Lords of the main

    (title and verse below transfer).

Jug.
Dawson.

331a

Young Cottagers

    (title above transfer).

Jug.
?'Garrison'.

332

The Young Poachers

    (title below transfer design).

Mug.
?Seaham.

BIBLIOGRAPHY

Anon.	'Some Brown Ware Potteries of the North of England', *Pottery Gazette*, July and August, 1916, pp.727-729 and pp.828-830.
Ball, W.R.	'Potteries of Sunderland and Neighbourhood', *Antiquities of Sunderland*, vol.VII, 1906, pp.35-52.
Bedford, J.	*Old English Lustre Ware*, 1965.
Bell, R.C.	*Tyneside Pottery*, 1971.
Bemrose, G.	*19th Century English Pottery and Porcelain. Guide to the Collection of English Lustre Ware* (Stoke-on-Trent Museum), 1949.
Buckley, F.	'Potteries on the Tyne and other Northern Potteries during the 18th century', *Archaeologia Aeliana,* 4th series, vol.IV, 1927, pp.68-82.
Buckmaster, M.A.	'English Lustre Ware', *Connoisseur*, vol.4, 1902, pp.195-9. 'English Lustred Earthenware, Copper, Silver and Gold, 1800-1900', *Connoisseur*, October, 1951, pp.107-112.
Chaffers, W.	*Marks and Monograms on European and Oriental Pottery and Porcelain*, 15th edition, 1965.
Corder, J.W.	*Wearside Potteries; Master Potters and Potteries of Sunderland and District* (n.d.). (In manuscript; can be consulted in Sunderland Central Reference Library).
Coysh, A.W. and Henrywood, R.K.	*The Dictionary of Blue and White Printed Pottery, 1780-1880,* 1982.
Cushion, J.P.	*Pocket Book of British Ceramic Marks*, 1983.
Drury, G.B.	'Sporting Pottery', *The Field*, 15th October, 1949, pp.546-547.
Des Fontaines, U.	*Wedgwood Fairyland Lustre*, 1975, Chap. I.
Gill, M.A.V.	'The Potteries of Tyne and Wear and their dealings with the Beilby/Bewick Workshop', *Archaeologia Aeliana,* 5th series, vol.IV, 1976, pp.151-170.
Godden, G.A.	*Encyclopaedia of British Pottery and Porcelain Marks*, 1968. *An Illustrated Encyclopaedia of British Pottery and Porcelain,* 1980.
Haggar, R.G.	*English Country Pottery*, 1950.
Harper, Mrs.	'Sunderland Lustre Motto Pottery', *Connoisseur*, vol.29, 1911, pp.34-37.
Hayden, A.	'Some Sunderland Mugs', *Connoisseur*, vol.9, 1904, pp.94-97.
Hodgdon, J.R.	*Collecting Old English Lustre*, 1937.
Honey, W.B.	*English Pottery and Porcelain*, 6th edition, 1975.
Houart, V.	*Easter Eggs: A Collector's Guide*, 1978.
Hughes, G.B.	*Collecting Antiques*, 1949. *Victorian Pottery and Porcelain*, 1959. 'Old English Lustre Ware', *Country Life,* 15th and 22nd November, 1946, pp.904-905 and pp.952-953. 'Sunderland Pottery', *Country Life,* 5th August, 1954, pp.434-436.
Hughes, G.B. and Hughes, T.	*Collectors Encyclopaedia of English Ceramics,* 1956.
Jewitt, L.	*Ceramic Art of Great Britain,* vol.II, 1878. 'Potteries on the Wear, the Tees, and the Mersey', *Art Journal,* new series, vol.VII, 1868, pp.253-254.
John, W.D., and Baker, W.	*Old English Lustre Pottery*, 1951.
Lewis G.	*Collector's History of English Pottery*, 1978.
Mankowitz, W. and Haggar, R.G.	*Concise Encyclopaedia of English Pottery and Porcelain,* 1957.
May, J. and J.	*Commemorative Pottery, 1780-1900,* 1972.
Miller, J. Jefferson II.	*English Yellow-Glazed Earthenware*, 1979.
Phillimore, J.	'A Famous Bridge in Pottery and Glass', *Apollo,* January and February, 1941, pp.6-9 and pp.35-37.

Rhead, G.W.   *The Earthenware Collector,* 1919.

Ritson, V.   'Sunderland Pottery', *Sunderland Echo,* 9th and 10th May, 1928, p.6.

Thorne, A.   *Pink Lustre Pottery,* 1926.

Towner, D.   *Creamware,* 1978.

Wallis, H.   'Old Masonic China and Glass', *Connoisseur,* vol.31, 1911, pp.238-244.

Walton, P.   *Creamware and Other English Pottery at Temple Newsham House, Leeds,* 1976.

Williams-Wood, C.   *English Transfer Printed Pottery and Porcelain,* 1981.